THE DAY OF VENGEANCE OF OUR GOD
and Earth's Golden Age Beyond

Dedication:
To loved ones whom I hope to meet in glory

THE DAY OF VENGEANCE OF OUR GOD

AND EARTH'S GOLDEN AGE BEYOND

A review of the Day of Vengeance and its relationship to
the Acceptable Year of the Lord and the Day of My Redeemed
as revealed in Scripture

DONALD C.B. CAMERON
BTh MA PhD Cert Ed

Foreword by Dr William Freel

JOHN RITCHIE LTD
CHRISTIAN PUBLICATIONS

40 Beansburn, Kilmarnock, Scotland

ISBN-13: 978 1 904064 35 0
ISBN-10: 1 904064 35 3

Copyright © 2007 by John Ritchie Ltd.
40 Beansburn, Kilmarnock, Scotland

Typeset by John Ritchie Ltd., Kilmarnock
Printed by Bell & Bain Ltd., Glasgow

Contents

Abbreviations

ASV American Standard Version (The American variant of the RV)

AV Authorised Version (Known in the USA as the King James Version).

NIV New International Version

NASB New American Standard Bible

JND New Translation by John N Darby

RV Revised Version

RSV Revised Standard Version

NKJV New King James Version

Foreword

Since the third century AD, Christians have been debating the sequence of events surrounding Christ's return. Through the years different methods of biblical interpretation have led to various explanations of the Bible's prophetic passages. Christians who agree on all the essential doctrines of the faith have been locked in verse-by-verse combat over who is right and who is wrong in the great eschatological debate.

The Day of Vengeance of our God, with the sub-title – **And Earth's Golden Age Beyond**, is now available and provides pragmatic and exegetical skill in the presentation of the Premillennial position. Dr Donald CB Cameron is an excellent scholar in the discipline of eschatology. His doctoral dissertation of over a hundred and thirty thousand words majored on a comparative evaluation of conflicting prophetic schools. His present book, however, is designed to assist those Christians who are searching for a reliable teaching based on a balanced biblical exposition.

There are a number of excellent principles, contained in this volume, that enable me to give an unreserved recommendation to the Christian community:

The Glossary of Terms.
This provides a basic vocabulary for the reader who may be confused with some of the terminology used in the teaching of prophecy. A few examples will help to whet the reader's appetite to study prophecy: Abomination of Desolation, Armageddon, Heptad, Replacement Theology etc, are all explained.

Eisegesis versus Exegesis.
Eisegesis was coined by Dr W Graham Scroggie, who, being so frustrated with preachers who habitually added to biblical text, cautioned

preachers to remember the words of Revelation 22.18: "For I testify to everyone who hears the words of the prophecy of this book: If anyone adds to these things, God will add to him the plagues that are written in this book". Dr Cameron in his exegesis of Revelation chapter 12 refuses to fall into the trap of naming the two witnesses. This wise methodology is consistently followed throughout his exposition.

Facing Knotty Questions.
Dr Cameron does not avoid puzzling or difficult passages. In Chapter One he examines Double and Multiple Fulfilments; in Chapter Two, Deviations and Misunderstandings; in Chapter Three Two Times Three-and-a-Half; and this careful approach to exegetical precision is followed meticulously in the content of his book.

Honouring Scripture.
Many books have been written on prophecy, but this one is special. To a greater extent than other authors, Dr Cameron also lays considerable tribute on the rest of the inspired Word in his expositionary presentation of prophecy. In highlighting his two key texts, namely Isaiah 61.1-3 and 63.3-4, he lays the foundation for a reverential approach to God's Word. From these verses he presents an important sequence: First, The Acceptable Year of the Lord; second, The Day of Vengeance of our God (The Day of Vengeance); third, The Year of the Redeemed. These themes form the kernel of the exposition.

An Evangelical Opportunity of Witness.
The Christians who purchase this book are making a wise investment. The book could play an important part in the salvation of friends and relatives. In his conclusion, Dr Cameron appeals for conversion! He asserts, "Whatever our denomination, church membership cannot save us; neither can a Christian family background, nor can our own good works, no matter how upright we may be. In the matter of our salvation we may have nothing of which to boast or glory 'save in the cross of our Lord Jesus Christ'".

Dr Cameron's book is balanced, sound and Scriptural, and deserves the widest possible circulation.

Dr William Freel, Dip Th, BD, MA, PhD has been a full-time Scottish evangelist and pastor of four well-known Baptist churches including Viewfield, Dunfermline and Duke Street, Richmond.

Acknowledgements

Firstly, I wish to thank Dr Roy Miller of Wingates, Northumberland, who a few years ago encouraged me to write a thesis on the Day of Vengeance of our God. Although much modified, with less academic content and more to appeal to a general readership, that thesis lies at the heart of this book.

Thanks are due to a number of knowledgeable friends who have been only a telephone call away for discussion or advice. Alphabetical order is the safest way to mention them.

Dr Theodore Danson Smith of Edinburgh I have known for three quarters of a lifetime as a student of prophecy and a writer whose opinions I can respect. As young men we were taught under the ministry of Dr James Sidlow Baxter.

Dr Bill Freel now of Inverness, past President of Prophetic Witness, when he heard that I was to have a few months of comparative inactivity whilst awaiting an operation, encouraged me to write this second book. I am honoured that he should have written the Foreword.

David Hoyle of Harrogate, currently Chairman of the Council of Prophetic Witness, who has lectured on prophecy as far afield as the Philippines, is an invaluable expert on Israel.

Rev Colin Le Noury, General Director of Prophetic Witness Movement and Rev Glyn Taylor, Editor of PW, have been glad to help with information as required.

My good friend and distant relative, Arthur McDonald (senior) of York Street Hall, Peterhead, who is among those 'who love His appearing', has been only a phone call away when I have needed someone to bounce ideas off.

Hamish McRae of Kinross-shire I have known for fifty-five years, and have even shared camping holidays with. He is always ready to give an off-the-cuff lecture on New Testament Greek and the comparative merits of different translations regarding more difficult texts.

Dr Michael Phelan of Sussex can be trusted to dig out the most obscure scholarly information when required, and to do this with incredible speed and efficiency.

Rev Keith Skelton, President of Prophetic Witness Movement International, has been a pastor of churches on both sides of the Atlantic. He preaches Bible prophecy with that all too rare mixture of compassion and fervour. He is a wise counsellor and friend, and a veritable Barnabas for encouragement.

With Rev Leslie Steele of Galashiels I have yet to discuss prophecy. But I want to thank him for his Christ-centred ministry, his courageous stand for Biblical principles and his sheer communication skills in profound exposition. In recent months, when my mind has followed prophetic highways and byways, he has given me a splendid balance of spiritual food.

CHAPTER ONE

Messiah's Three Phase Declaration

TWO SETS OF NEEDS

This book addresses two sets of needs, namely those of the believer and of the unbeliever. People in either group may have grave concerns about the future of this planet. Answers to their questions are provided from the Bible.

Among unbelievers there is often a genuine fear, sometimes even a degree of terror, about the future. They may have noticed that many churches do not offer answers to their questions, so it is hardly surprising that some turn to fortune tellers, astrologers and other occult sources, which are only too willing to oblige with their lies. Some try to forget it all by taking to drink or drugs. Others plunge themselves into well meaning but futile 'too little – too late' activities in order to try to 'save the planet'; one has to admire them for their dedication.

Believers may be puzzled. Over the past few decades there has been much teaching, re-enforced by triumphalist new songs, telling them of a golden age just around the corner, when the name of Jesus will be universally acclaimed. And yet the reality they see is one of looming ecological disasters, rampant immorality and violence, international terrorism, genocide and the explosion of militant Islam. This latter phenomenon in particular cannot be ignored.

Is the Bible wrong? Certainly not! Everything is on course in God's graciously revealed plans. But it is vital that unbelievers should know what steps God requires them to take for their eternal security, and equally important that believers should be better informed if they are to perform their much talked about 'salt and light' role.

In January 2007 a draft United Nations report by 2,500 eminent scientists was leaked. It issued a "Wake up call to the World" over environmental issues, and makes ominous reading. No doubt it made use of all the most reliable data available outside the Holy Scriptures. Christians have an infinitely more reliable source of data. Why then do so few churches issue wake up calls to the world? Could it be that many within those churches are less assiduous about analysing their data than the scientists? This ought not to be.

ATTITUDES TOWARDS PREDICTIVE PROPHECY

Within churches one encounters a variety of attitudes towards those many predictive prophecies of the Bible which have never been fulfilled to date, and in particular towards those concerning the future return of the Lord Jesus Christ, and events leading up to and beyond Armageddon.

There are those who have a simple but strong faith, which is the best kind of faith. They do not doubt God's promises, whether they fully understand them or not. To such people the prospect of the Lord's return is thrilling and motivating. Most would like to know more, but are also aware that there is work to be done in the time left. For them this book should prove helpful and cause few problems.

There are the timid Christians who are not disinterested and are probably aware of the fact that the Bible encourages the study of prophecy; but they are also aware that this is an area where there is inevitably some disagreement. They want to avoid controversy and feel that not taking sides is a commendable peacekeeping role. If they stay clear of the subject, they are likely to be less impressed by the priority that the Bible gives to it in terms of space and emphasis. It is easier to leave it to a few enthusiasts than to become personally involved.

There seem to be many believers who are quite prepared to believe in minor miracles today, but accept major ones only if they are kept at a respectable distance by two or three thousand years of history, or are so far in the future as to be of academic interest only. The possibility of any of the dramatic end-time events foretold in the Bible occurring in the foreseeable future is too overwhelming for them to contemplate.

Then there are the scoffers. These a few decades ago were a tiny minority within evangelical congregations; however their number seems to be growing. This is hardly surprising, because it is precisely what the Scriptures predict: "Scoffers will come in the last days, walking after their own lusts, and saying, 'Where is the promise of His coming?'" (II Pet 3.3-4). We will look at this passage in context later. Scoffing and spirituality are mutually exclusive.

Finally, there are those who welcome the 'nice' prophecies, but shun the 'nasty' ones. Perhaps they forget that it was Jesus Christ Himself who gave some of the most frightening ones. They may be a bit like those people who, having been given one of the old fashioned 'promise boxes', keep pulling out texts and returning them until they come upon one which they like. Their intensions may be honourable enough, but it is hardly faithful handling of the Word of God!

FLEE FROM THE WRATH TO COME!

Cartoonists used to love to portray grim looking old men, usually bearded and wearing raincoats, carrying sandwich boards. A favourite sandwich board caption was "The End Of The World Is Nigh". That is certainly not the message of this book. In fact, while we do predict on the basis of Bible prophecy that a terrible time of vengeance or tribulation lies ahead, we can guarantee that beyond it lies a long golden age, before God eventually brings this present world to an end.

Another favourite caption was "Prepare To Meet Your Doom". This is no more appropriate to our theme than the other one. While we do indeed have bad news, very bad news, we also have good news, very good news. God has provided an infallible means of escape from the Day of Vengeance through the death of His Son, the Lord Jesus Christ. This is not dependent upon our own good works or other merits. If we must be associated with one of these old captions, let it be "Flee From The Wrath To Come!" At the close of the book we will explain how we can do this.

Prophets of doom and gloom tend to be portrayed as cynical people, relishing in the bad news which they have to convey. But God's prophets, who were commissioned to pass on messages of judgment and even vengeance, were on the whole reluctant and inoffensive men. William Kelly perceptively entitles his commentary on Jeremiah, 'The Tender-hearted Prophet to the Nations'. Jonah was an exception. Teachers of

Bible prophecy are emphatically not prophets. Most are keenly aware of the awesome task they face in alerting others to what Jesus calls the "Signs of the Times". Many are naturally shy about bad news, this writer included, and are more enthusiastic about the good. However it is irresponsible and unfaithful to the Bible to deal with the one and not the other. There is nothing sinister about warning people of impending danger. Jesus had very severe words indeed for religious leaders who failed to observe and to draw attention to these signs.

We believe that we are living in an age when the Signs of the Times point very clearly to the near fulfilment of many prophecies, both cheering and ominous. In particular we believe that many of the signs which point to the near return of the Lord Jesus Christ are evident as never before. Jesus Himself was the greatest prophet of all. His Olivet Discourse, found with various degrees of coverage in Matthew, Mark and Luke, is one of His two longest addresses, whilst the last book of the Bible is stated to be "The Revelation of Jesus Christ". He, King of Kings, Lord of Lords and the Lamb of God, is pre-eminent there. If we love Him, we should hang upon His every word, particularly His final ones. If you do not yet love Him, please read on and discover more about the promised Day of Vengeance of our God and how to be "Counted worthy to escape all these things" (Lk 21.36). We have summarised some signs of the times in the closing chapter.

If you are a novice in the world of prophecy or a new Christian or as yet uncommitted, you will encounter what some might call technical jargon. We will try to keep this to the minimum, and have provided a short glossary at the end of the book. However it is patronising to assume that people object to learning a few new words. Every profession, trade, sport or hobby has its own jargon – sometimes many dozens of technical terms. People generally assume that it is normal to learn these, and we hope that our topic will be no exception. We are not dealing with trivialities, but with matters which deeply affect us all. We will offer a number of explanations, particularly in the first chapter, which we invite those who do not require them to pass over.

We make no apology for believing the Bible to be the inspired, unerring Word of God. We believe that what we will be encountering should re-inforce this view among those who are inclined to doubt. We will quote some passages, and provide references for others which readers may wish to turn to. A number of key verses will be quoted more than once, as different points have to be illustrated.

We are using the 'we' style, not because the book is written by a syndicate; it is not, but because there is something incredibly important to be shared. The author has the privilege of serving on the Council of Prophetic Witness Movement International, for whom he has written over a hundred articles, and knows that other Council and Movement members will agree with all except perhaps some fine details of this book; there is nothing unorthodox here.

THE TWO KEY VERSES

Let us now take a first look at the two passages in which we find the Day of Vengeance in context. Both are in the same section of Isaiah.

"The Spirit of the Lord God is upon Me, because the Lord has anointed Me to preach good tidings to the poor; He has sent Me to heal the brokenhearted, to proclaim liberty to the captives, and the opening of prison to those who are bound; to proclaim **the acceptable year of the Lord, and the day of vengeance of our God;** to comfort all who mourn, to console those who mourn in Zion" (Isa 61.1-3).

"I have trodden the winepress alone, and from the peoples no one was with Me, for I have trodden them in My anger, and trampled them in My fury; their blood is sprinkled upon My garments, and I have stained all My robes. For **the day of vengeance** is in My heart, and **the year of My redeemed** has come" (Isa 63.3-4).

The speaker indicated cannot be the prophet Isaiah, because the various functions listed can be performed only by the Messiah or by God. He is quoting prophetically, just as the Psalmist did (Ps 22.1) when he recorded Jesus' words from the Cross. The prophets of course did not realise that the Messiah was to be God in human flesh, but they were moved by the Holy Spirit to write. In the chapter 61 passage He tells us that He is anointed by the Lord (by God the Father in this context, because He cannot anoint Himself). This is consistent with basic Christian Trinitarian doctrine, which we uphold. The capital letters used in the NKJ version, are helpful, though not themselves inspired. Isaiah is merely the recording writer. Later we will find the most convincing possible confirmation from a well known passage in the New Testament, where Jesus quotes part of this text in a dramatic and significant way, unambiguously claiming the words for Himself.

Certain significant points seem to suggest themselves even at this stage of our investigation, including the listing of three important periods of time. Naturally they will need confirmation from other scriptures before they can be accepted as factual. Let us see what is becoming apparent.

All three of these periods will take place on earth. This ties in with Paul's statement in Acts 17.31, that God "has appointed a day on which He will judge the **world** in righteousness by the Man whom He has ordained." This is in contrast with the judgment of the saints for their service, which will be in Heaven, and with the Great White Throne for the unsaved after the present earth and its starry heavens have passed away (Rev 20.11).

We already have a sequence:-
1. The Acceptable Year of the Lord.
2. The Day of Vengeance of our God, or simply the Day of Vengeance.
3. The Year of My Redeemed.

Any who worry about a perceived break in continuity between the Isaiah 61 and 63 passages quoted should read on in chapter 61. The Speaker continues with further words of consolation and restoration after mentioning the Day of Vengeance; and the prophet adds, "And they shall rebuild the old ruins, they shall raise up the former desolations" (v.4). The scene is still very much an earthly one and conforms to what we shall later discover is revealed about the Year of the Lord's Redeemed. They did not occur during the Lord's earthly ministry.

Except where we are quoting Scripture, we propose to accord these terms capital letters throughout the book in order to highlight them. We will also accord capitals to certain other frequently found prophetic terms. When years and days do not have specific numbers appended, they may be taken simply as periods of longer or shorter duration. Thus we find this awesome "day" is to be sandwiched between two longer blessed "years". So we have in the above sequence a short period between two longer ones, or an awesome interlude between two epochs.

We already have observed that the first Messianic functions in the Isaiah 61 passage are associated with the Acceptable Year, whilst the latter ones seem to conform to the Year of the Lord's Redeemed, as these are 'good news'. Only the Day of Vengeance seems to stand out starkly on its own within the first passage as 'bad news'. Later we will study evidence that the Acceptable Year is rapidly drawing to a close, while the Day of Vengeance is drawing ever nearer.

Some of the questions which immediately arise and which require answers are:-

• What do these three terms actually mean?
• Are they uniquely applied to specific periods or are they general terms?
• Are they referred to elsewhere in Scripture?
• How long is each one, assuming it is possible to find out?
• Assuming they are consecutive, what precedes the Acceptable Year and what follows the Year of My Redeemed?
• How can a loving God be associated with a Day of Vengeance?

We will not necessarily tackle these questions in this sequence. Some will be investigated in later chapters. Readers familiar with these matters may wish to skim quickly through the remainder of this chapter, though we suggest that they do not skip it completely.

PROPHECY MUST BE HANDLED WITH PRAYER AND REVERENCE
We are handling the Word of God. We must establish certain rules for our study. This should make it more interesting, more quickly comprehensible and much more profitable. Some of these rules apply to the study of other great Bible themes; others apply only to the specialist nature of predictive prophecy. Some rules will need more explanation and expansion than others.

Whenever possible prophecy should be taken at face value. Of course some prophecies are symbolic. Often this is because heavenly or angelic scenes are being portrayed which are quite beyond our comprehension otherwise. Symbolism helps us to understand the gist of the message.

Sometimes it is because we are not intended at present to know more than one particular aspect of the message. However this is no excuse for allegorising what is perfectly comprehensible. Some 'difficult' visions are followed by simple interpretations; these must be taken at face value.

By the 4th Century AD, thanks to Clement of Alexandria, Origen, Augustine and others influenced by Platonism, Gnosticism and other Greek philosophy, much straightforward prophecy had come to be interpreted arbitrarily and allegorically. Believers ever since have been the losers. Augustine was the first major figure to apply one set of rules to the interpretation of prophecy and another to the rest of Scripture. This great thinker, whose conversion seems most convincing, became only selectively liberal. In later life he venerated Mary, taught that grace was available only via Rome and encouraged Constantine to persecute 'dissidents' who opposed the union of church and state. Compromise with any scriptural principle quickly leads to a slippery slope.

Students of Bible prophecy do not know all the answers; if any claim to, they should be shunned. We are privileged to know a great deal about the coming Day of Vengeance of our God, but there are still many areas which will be clear only to those undergoing those dreadful days. Prophecy must be handled with due care and reverence. It is inspired by the Holy Spirit. We have authority to state only what Scripture states, though we may legitimately express our prayerfully reached opinions, based on what is stated. Wise commentators know when to be cautious and when to be adamant. We may conclude that, as far as comprehension is concerned, there are three different categories of unfulfilled prophecy:-

- Those which make plain sense without any further study, although simple faith is required to accept even the obvious.
- Those which may be understood with diligent and prayerful study and by comparing different passages.
- Those which are intended to be understood fully only as the predicted event is taking place or just about to take place. It may be profitable to speculate here, but never to pontificate!

It is unhealthy to be preoccupied with Satan, demons and the occult world. However we do encounter these quite a lot in predictive prophecy.

Satan has everything to worry about here, and may be assumed to be an avid student of prophecy. We are dealing here with evil beyond our comprehension and cannot begin to understand why, in view of what God has foretold as inevitable, he does not desist from his ways. But it may be that preventing Satan from learning too much is one reason why God has not told us more. Blessing is attached to our study of prophecy. We learn this especially in the opening and closing verses of the book of Revelation. God does not reward laziness or bless apathy. He knows that sincere study of what He has predicted requires a little perseverance. He recognised the ancient Simeon and Anna (Lk 2.25-38) and will recognise our dedication if our motives are right.

Here is one reason for caution. Moses wrote: "There shall not be found among you...a soothsayer, or one who interprets omens, or a sorcerer... All who do these things are an abomination to the Lord" (Deut 18.10 & 12). Then he warned of false prophets, who evidently include not only those who deliberately prophesy falsely, but also those who take it upon themselves, for whatever reason, to issue prophecies of their own imagining. "The prophet who presumes to speak a word in My name, which I have not commanded him to speak...that prophet shall die... And if you say in your heart, 'How shall we know the word which the Lord has not spoken?'...If the thing does not happen or come to pass, the prophet has spoken presumptuously" (Deut 18.20-22).

These are solemn words indeed. It is the responsibility of congregations and their leaders to evaluate prophecies. What has become of the revivals which were loudly and unconditionally prophesied for our country two or three decades ago, but which never materialised? What about the cities which in the nineteen seventies and eighties were supposedly 'claimed for Christ', yet where churches are now being closed and mosques and temples built? According to the standards laid down through Moses, these prophecies were presumptuous. God was very severe with "those who prophesy out of their own heart...Woe to the foolish prophets" (Ezek 13.2-3). Even those false prophets who are well-meaning rather than malicious and who generally prophesy optimistic, encouraging words are roundly condemned by Scripture. Jeremiah and Ezekiel encountered them; their successors are around today. The false prophet's escape clause that lack of faith by others causes his prophecies to fail never avails if those prophecies were specific and unconditional.

The Old Testament provides us with case studies of Zedekiah the son of Chenaanah (I Kings 22.11 *et seq*) and Hananiah (Jer 28.1 *et seq*). There is no direct evidence that these men were deliberately trying to deceive. They simply presented their own views as being the word of the Lord, although they were arrogant and probably craved prestige. They sought the popular vote by proclaiming good news of their own initiative. Watch out for those who preach peace at any cost!

Peter also has solemn words for us. "We also have the prophetic word made sure, which you do well to heed as a light that shines in a dark place...No prophecy of Scripture is of any private interpretation, for prophecy never came by the will of man, but holy men of God spoke as they were moved by the Holy Spirit" (II Pet 1.19-21). Yet it was the same Peter who much earlier, when Jesus foretold His own death, protested and remonstrated with Him. He received the severest reprimand from His Lord of any disciple (Mk 8.33). Those whom we call Post-Millennialists claim to know better than Scripture, refusing to believe that the earth must undergo a future Day of Vengeance before any Year of the Lord's Redeemed; either that or they resort to that biggest disincentive to the study of prophecy, Preterism, which we will encounter later.

REVELATION IS PROGRESSIVE
Revelation in Scripture is progressive. Therefore we must expect greater clarity as we move from Genesis to Revelation. Thereafter the canon of Scripture is complete. We must not attempt to add to it.

Just as one can grasp the full significance of the Lamb, only if one goes right back to the Fall and to Abel, so one finds prophecies in the New Testament which cannot be fully comprehended without going back at least as far as the OT prophets and sometimes further. This is particularly true of the Lamb's role in Revelation. The many references in the Gospels, to Jesus as the Son of David, will be better appreciated if we start with the promises made to David by God through the prophet Nathan (II Sam 7.8-17).

The further we progress through the Bible, the more we find previous prophecies supplementing our understanding of new ones. We also find that prophecy relates to all the other major doctrines. One cannot study it in isolation, though it sometimes gives fresh slants, and can be instructional in unexpected ways.

DOUBLE AND MULTIPLE FULFILMENTS

Many prophecies have not only a main or final fulfilment, but have also had one or more partial fulfilments in the past. Saints down the ages have drawn comfort and reassurance from prophecies which they saw as being fulfilled in their day. We, with hindsight, perceive them to be still future. There is nothing wrong with this. Indeed, we can surely say confidently that the Holy Spirit carefully built in this flexibility. While, as we shall see in the next chapter, there is very little *specific* prophecy for the Church Age itself, there has been a wealth of provision by this means for persecuted believers over the centuries.

Certain prophecies where God has reserved the ultimate fulfilment for the Day of Vengeance, have been made by God's Holy Spirit very vivid to the suffering saints at various points in history. Notable is the comfort which the Reformation martyrs – and there were up to two million of these – derived from the identification of Mystery Babylon with the Vatican (Rev 17). Even some priests were upset about the obvious similarities. About 1500 AD a courageous Dominican monk called Savonarola led a mini-revival in Florence, confessing this identification publicly. He was brutally martyred in consequence. Yet we know that this prophecy is to have its final fulfilment in a latter day harlot religious monstrosity just before Christ's Coming in Power.

Two classical examples of dual fulfilment are found in Daniel and Joel. Daniel foretold the Abomination of Desolation in the Jerusalem Temple (9.27). At the time when Jesus gave His great Olivet Discourse, believing Jews were convinced that Daniel's prophecy had already been fulfilled in the 2nd Century BC by Antiochus Epiphanes. And so it had been! Yet Jesus declared that it had yet to happen at the end of the age; He gave a grave and very specific warning about it (Matt 24.15 and Mk 13.14).

Joel's great Pentecost prediction (2.28-32), quoted in Acts 2.17-21, demonstrates such a dual fulfilment. Peter declared that it was being fulfilled that very day. And so it was. But it has to be fulfilled again, when the entire prophecy will come to pass. The sun was not darkened nor the moon turned to blood at Pentecost, but they will be, following the opening of the sixth Seal (Rev 6.12). We will return to all these passages in different contexts, and note other examples of this prophetic phenomenon as we progress.

Sometimes there is a cut off point within a prophecy, at which it leaps hundreds or thousands of years to the next stage. No doubt the prophets themselves were unaware of this. They simply spoke as they were directed. The Holy Spirit was indicating a continuity of theme, despite the time lapse. We will in our next chapter see how Jesus spectacularly confirmed this principle with our two Isaiah texts.

We must beware of taking liberties and seeking obscure gaps to fit our ideas. Where Scripture makes it quite plain that two or more events take place at the same time, we must not separate them because we are uncomfortable with the implications. This is exceptionally important with the primary or final fulfilment of any prophecy.

FULFILLED PROPHECY THE KEY TO THE UNFULFILLED
We should use the many prophecies which were fulfilled whilst the Bible was still being written, as guidelines for anticipating how accurately the remaining prophecies will be fulfilled in the future. More often than not fulfilment was literal. Symbolism was the exception rather than the rule.

Admittedly as we look at the many episodes in the earthly life of Jesus, we do find a number of occasions when the disciples might have been excused for not having anticipated individual events. But prophecy is not only about informing us of what is about to happen. It is also – and this is very important indeed – to allow those experiencing fulfilment to realise that what is happening is what God has predicted. That is why we must be aware of prophecies which we do not yet fully understand.

The encounter with Jesus of the two broken-hearted disciples returning home to Emmaus has much to teach (Lk 24.13-32). "O foolish ones, and slow of heart to believe in all that the prophets have spoken! Ought not the Christ to have suffered these things and to enter His glory?" (vv.25-26). Jesus implied that they should have understood **as the signs became reality.**

When the Psalmist prophesied of Jesus, "They pierced My hands and My feet", (Ps 22.16), he was not merely suggesting cruelty. His prediction was precise, despite the fact that crucifixion would not be devised for hundreds of years. Micah specified Messiah's birthplace as Bethlehem Ephrathah (as opposed to the northern Bethlehem), so that there could be no mistake. This was no play upon words, such as the fact that Bethlehem means 'house of bread', nor did it signify something else obscure, open to guesswork. Micah was exact. When Zechariah foretold that their King would come riding on a donkey, he meant just that – a donkey. It was far, far more than a mere illustration of humility as has been suggested (Zech 9.9). And of course it was upon a donkey that the Saviour formally presented Himself to Jerusalem.

Events are prophesied for the Day of Vengeance which our generation, with its greater general knowledge and scientific expertise, can visualise much more clearly than our ancestors. Had God chosen to describe them in terms comprehensible to 21st Century nuclear physicists, meteorologists, marine biologists and environmentalists, they would have been totally incomprehensible to earlier Christians. Even now we have to be careful, for we cannot be certain how much of the coming judgment is direct miraculous intervention by God, and how much His allowing men to suffer from their own destructive technology.

CONDITIONAL AND UNCONDITIONAL PROPHECIES

We must differentiate between conditional and unconditional prophecies. Failure to do so can lead us into all sorts of difficulties, such as convincing ourselves that we can negotiate with God over the non-negotiable. Admittedly there are times when we can negotiate, as Abraham proved over Sodom. But practically all of the prophecies concerning the Day of Vengeance are unconditional. There are gracious conditions for individuals to seek salvation, but none to divert God's wrath from persistently unrepentant mankind.

Immediately after the Fall God made a prophecy to the serpent, evidently within the hearing of Adam and Eve. The woman's Seed was to bruise the serpent's head. This promise was unconditional, despite a long time lag; "When the fullness of the time had come, God sent forth His Son, born of a woman, born under the law, to redeem those who were under the law..." (Gal 4.4-5). Satan could not stop that happening, though he tried.

The long list of blessings and curses given by God to Israel through Moses is conditional prophecy (Deut 28.1 et seq). The conditions for blessing were broken. Here God gave further chances, some curses were temporarily lifted as repentance and revival occurred. But ultimately the curse recorded in vv.64 & 65 was invoked; the nation was scattered and has had no rest, "but the Lord will give you a trembling heart, failing eyes, and anguish of soul". The accuracy of these prophecies as fulfilled in the subsequent history of the Jews is remarkable – a study in its own right. There are a number of major prophecies concerning Israel in particular, which are restricted by 'until' or 'not until' rather than by 'unless'

A most significant such conditional prophecy was given by Jesus a few days before His crucifixion. To Jerusalem He said: "You shall see Me no more till you say, 'Blessed is He Who comes in the name of the Lord'" (Matt 23.39). This was conditional regarding timing; 'till' was the key word. Zechariah chapter 12 tells us how and when that condition will eventually be met. In the meantime, prayer for Israel is entirely appropriate. So is the evangelisation of Jews. Every saved Jew in this present age immediately becomes a member of the Church. But comprehensive national recognition will not and cannot take place until Jesus Christ returns in power and "They will look on Me Whom they have pierced." (Zech 12.10). So here the event is unconditional, as confirmed by Zechariah, but the timing is conditional.

We must not apply faulty human logic to these matters. The Bible does not teach a kismet philosophy. We must not be detracted from our present work for the Lord by the inevitability of those things which God has declared to be unconditional. But we should be aware of our limitations. This is not defeatism. It is obedience.

The fact that covenants were broken does not mean that God had not foreseen this eventuality, or that He was compelled to provide alternatives as afterthoughts, an accusation often made in ignorance; we will give an example in the next chapter. But there is always a cost for the individuals who break the covenants. This lesson is emphasised in Psalm 89.28 et seq: "My mercy I will keep for him forever...", then God warns of the consequences of violation: "If his sons forsake My law...then I will visit their transgression with the rod...". But finally He reassures David that, despite this, He will never break His covenant. "It shall be established forever like the moon, even like the faithful witness in the sky".

THE CHURCH AND ISRAEL

When we use the term 'the Church' without further qualification, we are referring to "the church of God which He purchased with His own blood" (Acts 20.28). The Church is the body and espoused Bride of Christ, its precise membership being known only to God. Membership depends entirely on redemption through faith in the finished work of Jesus Christ on Calvary, following repentance, which acknowledges our need of Him. It is not dependent upon race, status or denominational label; it leaves no room for personal pride, being freely provided by "God, who so loved the world" to all who will accept it.

When we talk of 'Israel' the sense will generally be obvious, because it will refer either to the people or to the modern nation state. The name, which means 'having power with God' or 'God's warrior', was given by God to Jacob; thus his descendents became the Children of Israel, Israelites or simply Israel. From David's time onwards it was applied to the ten Northern tribes, who broke away from the Davidic line of kings. From the time of the Exile, Israelites were generally known as Jews. In the New Testament the title applies to the whole Jewish race; and of course since 1948 it has been the name of the nation occupying part of the Holy Land. The term 'Israel of God' (Gal 6.16) occurs only once in the Bible, when it applies only to regenerate or believing Jews, as opposed to unbelieving Jews. It does not apply to the Church, though many Protestants have, on the basis of the tiniest percentage of the Scriptural evidence available, annexed it for themselves.

We have already noted unfulfilled unconditional prophecies regarding Israel. We must not exclude Israel from God's future plans. God has sidelined His ancient people, whilst the Church, which includes saved Jews, has occupied the mainline, so to speak. But they are still God's people; Jerusalem is still His city. "Has God cast away His people? Certainly not!" (Rom 11.1). Both in Jeremiah and Hosea we find Israel cast aside from God's purposes for spiritual harlotry. Yet within the same prophetic books she is assured in the most affirmative ways, guaranteed by God Himself, that she will one day be most graciously reinstated and restored.

The teaching that the Church has taken over all the roles and privileges of Israel forever is called Replacement Theology. It throws understanding of much of Old Testament prophecy into total confusion and does nothing to help us to understand Revelation. Since Pentecost the 'middle wall of partition' between Jew and Gentile has been broken down. Jews and Gentiles alike are reconciled to God in one body through the cross (Eph 2.14-16). But God still has plans for His currently unrepentant and wayward Jewish nation. History and the Bible together witness eloquently to the unparalleled miraculous preservation of a race which, in theory, should be classed along with the Hittites, Carthaginians and Assyrians as a dead nation. To 'spiritualise' all the prophetic references to Jerusalem is surely one of the most unspiritual things we can do. These matters are close to the heart of God. History demonstrates that it is not unfair to describe Replacement Theology as a Charter for Anti-Semitism.

Very few Replacement Theologians devote much time to latter day predictive prophecy. It is not difficult to understand why, because their position presents them with so many enigmas. We would respectfully suggest that any reader still inclined towards this stance should thoughtfully read Ezek 39.21-29, a passage to which we will be returning in a different context in chapter 4. Here we find that:-

- The terms of the prophecy are unconditional.
- It follows God's judgment of the nations (v.21).
- The whole house of Israel will be recovered and reunited (v.25) unlike as at the return from Babylon
- God will have brought them back from their enemies' lands (v.27).
- None of Israel will be left in captivity (v.28).
- God will pour out His Spirit on Israel, who will at last recognise Him (vv.28-29).

There is much else in this passage which simply does not fit in with the Church which, according to some, has annexed all Israel's promises. My book, 'Apocalypse Facts and Fallacies', deals with these matters at length.

While we strongly oppose Replacement Theology, we must avoid the trap of being so besotted with Israel that we believe that she can do no wrong. God does not believe this, as the most cursory reading of the Bible will confirm; but He still loves them, and so should we. Increasing Anti-Semitism demands that we should take a courageous stand if we are on the Lord's side. However it is fair to say that, by their persecution of the early Church, Jews did much to bring Anti-Semitism upon themselves, particularly once the Roman Empire formally embraced Christianity and serious apostasy set in. Presenting an imbalance as a counter-reaction to the Replacement view does nothing to help win Jews for Christ or to help those who have been won to understand that their membership of the Church of Jesus Christ is paramount.

APPROACH TO REVELATION

Dr John F Walvoord in the preface to his commentary on Revelation states: "The expositor of the Revelation is inevitably forced to choose one of the systems of interpretation which have emerged in the history of the church as a proper approach to this last book of the Bible". (The Revelation of Jesus Christ). This is sound advice. In his introduction he lists the main options and opts, as we do, for the Futuristic one.

In our book we will adhere to the Futuristic interpretation of Revelation from Chapter 4 onward. Naturally we will not confine our study to Revelation, although that will provide more source material than any other book, because this last God-given apocalypse or unveiling is the one which provides the most information of how other prophecies fit into a sequence or framework. At this juncture, however, let us simply say of the Futurist overview that:-

- It is consistent with the frequent injunctions of Scripture to study and understand these matters, and to look expectantly for the return of the Lord Jesus Christ.

- It allows for natural rather than allegorical understanding of many other passages. Maximum allegorical interpretation, which underpins other approaches and where the text itself provides no further clues, leads to endless speculation; the wilder the imagination the more fantastic the interpretations.

- It portrays the Lord's return as being potentially and realistically ever imminent. It imposes no pre-conditions on His immediate return.

- It is consistent with the contrast between His coming **for** and His coming **to** – His coming for his saints to take them to glory at the

Rapture and His subsequent return to earth with His saints at the end of the Great Tribulation – our next chapter explains.

- It recognises the inescapable fact that the world is getting worse rather than better, and that it increasingly fits Jesus' description of a latter day scenario comparable with the days of Noah and of Lot.

- It provides for 'Satan's last fling' – his final challenge to God, the appearance and activities of his false messiah or Antichrist, the destruction of both Mystery Babylon and Babylon the Great, a world-wide rebellion against Christ, means of individual repentance and salvation and a manifestation of Divine wrath. It confirms that when Satan is at last bound he will no longer be able to prowl around as a lion.

- It is the only approach which recognises a future thousand year righteous rule, when 'the head that once was crowned' with thorns' will indeed be crowned with glory on earth. His at last will be the highest place that earth, as well as Heaven, affords.

- It acknowledges a future end to this old planet, a final judgment of the unsaved and a glorious eternal state, where "the Lamb is in the midst".

Other overviews, we believe, fall short on one or more of these conditions.

The Book of Revelation alternates between Heaven and earth. What happens in Heaven was more difficult for the Apostle John to describe and thus for us to understand. Much there had to be shown in visionary form, but nevertheless depicted facts rather than mere principles. Also in Heaven there are no timescales, certainly as we know them, but there are sequences; and those sequences may dictate sequences on earth, though not necessarily at the same apparent intervals that John saw them. Thus, for instance, while the opening of the Seals signals events which will take place over a few years, their actual opening may have appeared to John to happen in very quick succession.

Some descriptions are given from a heavenly point of view and may look entirely different upon earth. However strange they may seem, these people and events will be real enough. God sees the Antichrist in his true light, in other words as a hideous monster; yet to the majority of people upon earth he will be perceived as a brilliant statesman. God sees Satan as a dragon seeking to devour the seed of the Woman, namely Jews; but all that people are likely to be aware of will be a massive increase in unrelenting Anti-Semitic activity. When we come to these passages in later chapters we will perceive the contrasts.

However we must beware of 'interpreting' or seeking hidden meanings in prophesied earthly happenings which make perfectly good sense in the language in which they are described. We adhere to the principle, attributed to the Scottish theologian Dr Horatius Bonar, that where the plain sense makes sense we should seek no other sense. Failure to observe this principle often marks the cut-off point between the wisdom of God and the wisdom of the world, between conservative and liberal theology and between believing the Bible and merely tinkering with it. This also applies to much of Daniel and parts of Ezekiel and Zechariah.

PROPHETIC STUDY MUST BE CHRISTOCENTRIC
As we proceed with our studies we will see Jesus of Nazareth inaugurate the Acceptable Year of the Lord (Lk 4.19). We will find Daniel troubled by his visions, which revealed what was completely unknown hitherto, "One like the Son of Man coming with the clouds of heaven" (Dan 7.13-15). We shall find the future surviving inhabitants of Jerusalem looking on the One whom they pierced (Zech 12.10). We shall see Jesus identified as Jehovah God, going forth to war, coming with His saints, and His feet standing on the Mount of Olives (Zech 14.3-5). In verse 9 of the same chapter we shall read of how He shall be King over all the earth.

In His Olivet address (Matt 24, Mk 13 and Lk 21), we shall find Jesus telling of His own omnipotent future actions. In Revelation we shall see Him as the One Who is both Lion of the Tribe of Judah and the 'Lamb as though it had been slain' opening the Seals which are to lead to the Day of Vengeance of our God (Rev 5). And so we could go on. The Lord Jesus is always central.

We are going to see much of Jesus Christ as the righteous Judge. It is He who from Heaven will either initiate or authorise events on earth during the Day of Vengeance. But we must be aware that Heaven is outside the sphere of time and that Jesus is even now in eternity. Remembering this may help us to understand better the apparent timing enigmas in the constant interactions between Heaven and Earth, especially as found in Daniel and Revelation. We will refer back to this.

We, the Church, have many important responsibilities. But we are only Christ's ambassadors, not His vice-regents. "Will a man rob God?" asks Malachi (3.8). We must not imagine that we can usurp the roles which the Father has reserved for the Son. His must be all the glory. Let us strive to obtain crowns from His hand, so that we, like the elders of Revelation 4, may be able to cast them at His feet.

THE CONCEPT OF VENGEANCE

After the Acceptable Year of the Lord comes the Year of My Redeemed. But between them, inevitably, inexorably, irresistibly must come the Day of Vengeance of our God. The Day of Vengeance is the next short but blackest chapter in the world's history. Later we will see that even then there will be cause for rejoicing. But that will be in Heaven, regarding certain events on earth. As yet we are not sufficiently heavenly minded to accept comfortably the righteousness of vengeance – even God's vengeance.

We find the same Hebrew term for the Day of Vengeance in Isa 34.8: "It is the Day of the Lord's Vengeance, the year of recompense for the cause of Zion." Now, while there may be an interim application of those words, the primary application is still future and conforms to the central part of Revelation. Note for instance v.2, "The indignation of the Lord is against all nations, and His fury against all their armies", and v.4 "All the host of heaven shall be dissolved, and the heavens shall be rolled up like a scroll." This of course refers to the atmospheric heavens. We will return to this chapter of Isaiah later. The "year of recompense" equates to the Year of His Redeemed.

Many Christians simply feel uncomfortable with the idea of a Day of Vengeance and would either try to find a way of deflecting it, which is patently impossible, of postponing it indefinitely, or of denying it. Some are aware of the fact that vengeance is not 'politically correct', and therefore worry that it might hinder the work of preaching the Gospel. The history of the great revivals actually teaches us precisely the opposite; but that is largely forgotten. Jesus talked of Hell more than anyone else in the Bible, but Christians dare to know better. Is this not a sign of the times?

So what is this 'vengeance' which Isaiah foretold, but which Jesus carefully avoided mentioning at the start of His earthly ministry, yet prophesied at its close? Before we consider the precise meaning of the word, let us emphasise that it is not synonymous with 'judgment'. Certainly vengeance is a category of judgment, but judgment can have many meanings other than vengeance. Here are a few instances of vengeance in the Old Testament.-

- "Take vengeance for the children of Israel on the Midianites. Afterward you shall be gathered to your people...... take vengeance for the Lord on Midian" (Num 31.2-3). The world would do well to heed these words of God to Moses. He will yet take vengeance on the enemies of His ancient people, His Church and His tribulation saints. God specifically authorised this vengeance, as was His right.
- "He will avenge the blood of His servants" (Deut 32.43).
- "Strengthen me, I pray, just this once, O God, that I may with one blow take vengeance on the Philistines for my two eyes!" (Judg 16.28). The speaker was of course Samson. And the location? Gaza! God answered that prayer, so it must have been His vengeance too.
- "Be strong, do not fear! Behold, your God will come with vengeance, with the recompense of God; He will come and save you." (Isa 35.4).
- "For His plan is against Babylon to destroy it, because it is the vengeance of the Lord, the vengeance for His temple" (Jer 51.11). There are four mentions of vengeance regarding Babylon in Jeremiah 50 and 51. There are applications both to ancient Babylon and Babylon the Great, about which we will learn more from Revelation 18.

In the New Testament, in addition to *antapodoma*, we find the equally strong Greek word *ekdikesis* for vengeance, with the verb *ekdikeo* for avenge. Note its use in the following:-

- "For these are (the) days of vengeance, that all things that are written may be fulfilled" (Lk 21.22). This is part of the Olivet Discourse. Jesus is talking about the latter days – beyond the Acceptable Year. Most Greek texts do not have the definite article here.

- "When the Lord Jesus is revealed from heaven with His mighty angels, in flaming fire taking vengeance on those who do not know God, and on those who do not obey the gospel of our Lord Jesus Christ" (II Thess 1.7-8). The scenario here is Armageddon.
- In Jude v.7 vengeance is applied to Sodom and Gomorrah.

Unger's Bible Dictionary defines vengeance as "Punishment inflicted in return for an injury suffered; retribution; often passionate or unrestrained revenge." Instances of human revenge are then listed; these are not relevant to our study. It then adds: "When vengeance is predicted of the Lord it must be taken in the better sense of righteous punishment." Of the Greek *ekdikesis*, as found in Lk 21.22, it says that the word expresses the ideas of executing righteous judgement, vindicating one from wrongs or avenging an injured person. Lk 18.7 and Acts 7.24 and 28:4 are also quoted.

MORALITY AND EXCLUSIVENESS OF GOD'S VENGEANCE

"The idea that God is a 'God who avenges' (Ps 94.1) troubles some. Is not vengeance evil? How can a trait that we deplore in human beings be appreciated in God?" (Lawrence O Richards, Expository Dictionary of Bible Words).

What is wrong of course is the human concept of God, and the failure to understand the implications of His incomparable holiness. If we fully understood the supreme cost to God of Calvary, we might appreciate better the awfulness of the sin from which Jesus Christ came to redeem us and the dreadful intensity of the burden of sin which He bore for us. We would also understand better why failure to accept His Son is such a heinous crime in His sight. "It is a fearful thing to fall into the hands of the living God" (Heb 10.31). His vengeance is doubly righteous inasmuch as He has provided a way of escape, which is often rejected. Scripture furnishes us with ample evidence of divine patience before vengeance is applied. He is "longsuffering toward us, not willing that any should perish but that all should come to repentance" (II Pet 3.9).

While God certainly assigns the duty of punishing, He is very strict in reserving for Himself the right to execute vengeance. He may sometimes delegate it; but it is never the prerogative of any person to assume this authority for himself. Only God has the essential holiness and perfect knowledge.

The American Tract Society's Dictionary says that vengeance, in Deut 32.35; Rom 12.19; Heb 10.30 and Jude 1.7, "means retributive justice – a prerogative of God with which those interfere who seek to avenge themselves". In other words, vengeance by any other person is a challenge to divine rights. We must conclude therefore that vengeance is not in itself wrong. It is simply that nobody other than God is qualified to exercise it. Thus we understand better why God says: "Vengeance is Mine and recompense" (Deut 32.35). This is quoted by Paul and the writer to the Hebrews: "Beloved, do not avenge yourselves, but rather give place to wrath, for it is written, 'Vengeance is Mine, I will repay' says the Lord" (Rom 12.19), and "We know Him who said, 'Vengeance is Mine, I will repay'" (Heb 10.30).

The Psalmist cries: "O Lord God, to whom vengeance belongs – O God, to whom vengeance belongs, shine forth! Rise up, O Judge of the earth; render punishment to the proud, Lord, how long will the wicked, how long will the wicked triumph?" (Ps 94.1). This cry is not unique in Scripture. We find similar pleas, especially elsewhere in the Psalms and in Revelation. God recognises the righteousness of such appeals, and He will answer in His own good time. The Day of Vengeance of our God is coming. Even the imprecatory Psalms are part of Holy Scripture.

We dare not overlook, however, God's reluctance to execute vengeance until there is no other way, until calls for repentance have been exhausted. To Jonah, Nineveh was the cruel hereditary oppressor of his own nation; his human sentiments were understandable. But consider God's admonition to Jonah, who had built himself a little booth from which to have a grandstand view of what he hoped would be the destruction of the city. "Should I not pity Nineveh, that great city, in which are more than one hundred and twenty thousand persons who cannot discern between their right hand and left, and also much livestock?" (Jonah 4.11). Nineveh's stay of execution lasted around two hundred and fifty years. Jonah had complained to God: "I know that You are a gracious and merciful God, slow to anger and abundant in lovingkindness, One who relents from doing harm" (4.2). The prophet was quoting God's revelation of Himself to Moses (Ex 34.6-7).

The stay of execution for Sodom and Gomorrah, which Abraham had negotiated with God, never materialised. But it would have done had a mere ten righteous people been found within (Gen 18.32 et seq). The negotiated condition was not met. The fate of those cities has become proverbial. Jesus Himself referred to it (Matt 10.15, Lk 17.29 etc). Jude said that it was vengeance (1.7) - avertable but not averted. The coming Day of Vengeance of our God cannot be averted; God's holiness and justice demand that it must come.

The Cross of Calvary is rightly described by the Scottish hymn writer, Elizabeth Clephane, as the "trysting place where heaven's love and heaven's justice meet". Because He is Almighty God, He always had the right to exercise vengeance. Because He willingly became the Victim of the greatest sacrifice, and the centre of the greatest outpouring of love of all time and eternity, His vengeance is overwhelmingly just.

Before we leave this subject, we might remind ourselves that not all suffering is the direct or even indirect consequence of the sin of the sufferer. Job's companions or 'comforters' had fallen into a trap. As far as they were concerned, Job's ordeals were the result of his own sin, though, unlike many today, at least they were careful not to blame God. But God was not pleased with them. In the closing section of the book God addresses Eliphaz the Temanite: "My wrath is aroused against you and your two friends, for you have not spoken of Me what is right, as My servant Job has" (Job 42.7). Subsequently, after Job had prayed for his friends "the Lord restored Job's losses...the Lord blessed the latter days of Job more than his beginning" (vv.10-12). The disciples also had to learn not to jump to the wrong conclusions in attributing cause and effect in suffering. When they enquired whether a certain man's blindness was the result of his own or his parents' sin, Jesus' response was, "Neither this man nor his parents sinned, but that the works of God should be revealed in him" (Jn 9.3). Our inability to judge objectively in these matters gives us all the more reason to be thankful that our Father in Heaven has retained exclusively for Himself the prerogative of vengeance.

OUR PROPHETIC STANCE
The book is written with conviction from a Pre-Millennial stance, not

nowadays the most widely found school of prophecy, but the most common stance among those who take the predictive prophecy of the Bible seriously and, to use Paul's words, who love the Lord's appearing. While we firmly believe that the main facts of latter day prophecy are quite clear and propose to expound these, we re-emphasise that there are some details which will not be fully understood until the prophesied events are about to happen or are actually taking place. It is neither clever nor responsible to be adamant about such matters; caution must sometimes be exercised. We have not avoided such issues, but have discussed a number of the more important of them and given considered opinions. The existence of such questions in no way undermines the authority of Scripture; rather the opposite.

Pre-Millennialism, or Chiliasm to use an old term, was the view held by many early Church fathers. Later, as non-literalism grew, it was gradually replaced by an apathetic Amillennialism. A minority of the Reformers revived and preached the old truths, but most were too pre-occupied with other immensely important issues. The story that it was invented by John Nelson Darby, who based it upon the teachings of the Jesuit Lacunza is nonsense. Many from the 17th Century revived the preaching of the Rapture of the Church. However it was never a central topic in those optimistic centuries, when many assumed the Bible to be wrong, thinking that the earth was actually getting better in preparation for the Lord's return.

Certainly Darby in the eighteen forties and fifties made so great an impact by his exposition of prophecy, that many attempts, some out of ignorance and some out of dishonesty, have been made to try to discredit him by associating him with those with whom he used to debate prophecy in his early days, but who went astray later in fundamental doctrines. We may not agree with quite everything he said about the latter days, but must acknowledge that he more than anyone else under God was instrumental in inspiring the huge rise of interest in prophecy throughout the English speaking world, which in turn led to there being so many influential figures, both in public life and in evangelical circles, available to support the 1917 Balfour Declaration and a Jewish homeland. The subsequent falling off and scoffing is itself a proof of the Lord's near coming.

We are concerned about the other two leading schools of prophetic interpretation, not because of rivalry or rancour, and certainly not because of any feeling of spiritual superiority. But we are unhappy that, when the need for an intelligent awareness of the signs of the times is greater than ever, teaching which simplifies end-time prophecies is on the increase. Both A- and Post Millennialism tend to allocate study time for prophecy in inverse proportion to its coverage in Holy Scripture.

Just as in New Testament times, Pharisees and Sadducees, who doctrinally had nothing in common, could lay aside their differences when it suited them, so A- and Post-Millennialists can forget the fact that they are totally incompatible with one another, and present a united front against Pre-Millennialism. This is much more at leadership, than at 'grass-roots' level, as preachers of prophecy bear witness from feedback from congregations. Again we are taken back to New Testament conditions. Pre-Millennialism is not 'sophisticated' and, worse, it challenges the status quo!

As apathy towards prophecy has increased, and some formerly conservative Bible colleges have been infiltrated by creeping modernism, evangelical congregations have veered towards the scoffers and welcomed schools of prophetic interpretation which are more acceptable to liberals. Readers who doubt this should ask current students whether Pre-Millennialism is given as fair and unbiased a coverage as other schools of interpretation. Perhaps in the academic world the miraculous element of Pre-Tribulationism, with an emphasised early Rapture, requires rather more courage than the blander options. These are generalisations; there are splendid exceptions. Moreover we know many fine Christians with whom we would see eye to eye on all doctrines other than this.

While we interpret literally all prophecy which is not overtly visionary, symbolic or allegorical, we would stretch the definition of 'literal' to allow for modern weaponry such as tanks and firearms to be represented in the Bible by horses and spears, and so on as appropriate. These prophecies had to make sense for many centuries. God would have understood, but readers would not have done so.

CHAPTER TWO

The Day of Vengeance Postponed

HOW TO PROCEED

In this chapter we will look at the inauguration of the Acceptable Year and consider what it involves; then we will see how the Acceptable Year has proceeded and what changes if any there have been during its course. Finally we will see how the Acceptable Year has to end. As we believe we are now very near the end of this age, this will be important. If we do not understand the significance of our present two thousand year old age, we are unlikely to be able to see how the Bible's many as yet unfulfilled and unconditional prophecies are to fit in. It would be easy indeed to digress profitably into several chapters to cover the Acceptable Year; however bearing in mind the title of our book, we will have to suffice with a single chapter.

There is a tendency to assume that the Church Age and Acceptable Year of the Lord are identical. But this is not so, because Jesus clearly announced that the Acceptable Year was starting there and then at the beginning of His earthly ministry, whereas the Church Age started at Pentecost. The crowds of pilgrims from the far flung corners of the Roman Empire, whom Peter addressed at Pentecost, were Dispersion or diaspora Jews. Gentiles were made welcome a little later.

John in the introduction to his Gospel wrote of Jesus: "He came to His own, and His own did not receive Him. But as many as received Him, to them He gave the right to become children of God, to those who believe in His name" (Jn 1.11-12). We are about to see in Luke chapter 4 Jesus formally coming to His own, the lost sheep of the tribe of Israel. We Gentiles in the Church are included in the "as many as received Him".

THE MESSIANIC MISSION STATEMENT

Why did Jesus not include His death and resurrection in His announcement of the things He was about to do? Why? Because they were unplanned? Certainly not! They are critical elements of God's eternal plan of salvation. Many of the three hundred plus OT prophecies concerning His first coming referred to them, particularly to His death. No. He did not start telling even the disciples about those events until the leaders of the nation had had an opportunity to accept Him under the terms of His Nazareth declaration. Only after His rejection, which was foreseen in God's overview, did the portent of these other matters become comprehensible. Later, on the evening of His resurrection day, He asked, "Ought not the Christ to have suffered these things and to enter into His glory?" (Lk 24.36). Of course He should. But at the beginning of His ministry, His declared immediate objectives were more limited. Had Jesus announced at that stage His future rejection, He would have detracted from the genuine and open offer He was making to His own, and would have pre-empted the hostile reaction of the religious leaders to His ministry.

In Chapter 1 we printed what we said was Isaiah's prophetic quote of the Messiah. We now substantiate this claim by turning to Luke's account of Jesus' reading from Isaiah 61.

"So Jesus came to Nazareth, where He had been brought up. And as His custom was, He went into the synagogue on the Sabbath day, and stood up to read, and He was handed the book of the prophet Isaiah. And when He had opened the book, He found the place where it was written: 'The Spirit of the Lord is upon Me, because He has anointed Me to preach the Gospel to the poor. He has sent Me to heal the brokenhearted, to preach deliverance to the captives and recovery of sight to the blind, to set at liberty those who are oppressed, to preach **the acceptable year of the Lord.**' Then He closed the book, and gave it back to the attendant and sat down. And the eyes of all who were in the synagogue were fixed on Him. And He began to say to them, 'Today this Scripture is fulfilled in your hearing'" (Lk 4.16-21).

The contrast between this and Isaiah's prophetic quote lies of course in Jesus' abrupt but deliberate and dramatic halt in His reading, indicating that while the Acceptable Year of the Lord was now being inaugurated, the Day of Vengeance and subsequent events in the prophecy were being postponed.

All eyes were fixed on Him in the Nazareth synagogue. And no wonder, when we think of the drama of that moment, the implications and the Person of the Speaker! Every eye will again be fixed upon Him when He comes in a different role. "Behold, He is coming with clouds, and every eye will see Him..." (Rev 1:7). Here He came in humility. But it is 'this same Jesus', whether in Nazareth or in future glory.

Jesus was handed the scroll of the prophet Isaiah. Normally when a reader or actor quotes poetry or prose, he or she is merely echoing the original, be it Scott, Wordsworth or Shakespeare. But this is different. It was Isaiah who was the echo and Jesus who is the Original. As we shall see, Jesus exercised the right and authority to slip in an addendum and then to cut short His reading at an opportune juncture.

From the text, we conclude that it was not the first time that He had read in the local synagogue, where He had been a regular worshipper. As a non-professional person, He would have qualified by His character and reputation rather than by His calling. He was there, as far as the synagogue rulers were concerned, simply as an honest and devout local man.

It is not surprising that it is Luke who recorded this incident. Luke is the Gospel writer who portrays Jesus as the Son of Man. His humanity had been demonstrated immediately before this Nazareth incident, when He had been tempted for forty days in the wilderness. But His divinity had also been confirmed. For He rebuked Satan with the words, "You shall not tempt the Lord your God" (Lk 4.12). Satan was in no doubt whatsoever about His deity, but was seizing upon the opportunity of His voluntary human frailty. Jesus had resisted the temptation which would have given Him the world's adulation without going to the Cross. "All this authority I will give you, and their glory; for this has been delivered to me..." (Lk 4.6). His humanity had been tested, but so had the sinlessness, which qualified Him to be our Substitute and Sinbearer. He had not been found wanting. Even in Jesus' opening quotation of Isaiah we see the three Persons of the Godhead.

By announcing that this was being fulfilled within their hearing, Jesus in His reading identified Himself as the Anointed One, the Messiah or Christ. Before His temptation Jesus had been baptised both with water by John, and also with the Holy Spirit – by man and by God. There were many witnesses to the voice from Heaven at His baptism, though apparently He alone saw the Spirit descending as a dove (Matt 3.16-17).

Jesus was given the Spirit "without measure" (Jn 3.34). He alone was anointed to all three offices – Prophet, Priest and King. This indeed was the sequence in which He would begin to fill each. At Nazareth He was proclaiming Himself firstly Prophet (Deut 18.15). There is also in the text an allusion to His priestly office, inasmuch as salvation is implied. Also, whilst He markedly stopped short of Isaiah's statement which referred to His future Kingship, the issuing of a proclamation might have been considered a kingly role. But the emphasis on this occasion was on His role as the Prophet, whose words Isaiah had 'pre-iterated' more than seven hundred years before. He was in fact to be a miracle working Prophet, like Elijah or Elisha. The difference was that all Jesus' miracles were beneficial, whereas some of theirs were judgmental.

THE OPENING ANNOUNCEMENT
These words are among the most significant spoken in human history. As we have noted, Jesus was giving His terms of reference at the outset of His public ministry, and He was doing so in, so to speak, His parish church and in front of His own congregation, friends and no doubt family!

We have space to look only briefly at those statements which precede the announcement of the Acceptable Year of the Lord, but we dare not skip them completely. There is some debate about the exact significance and scope of each sentence. All can relate to at least one Messianic prophecy. The primary or obvious meaning must be paramount, but there seems to be legitimate scope for reading secondary applications as well, such as the poor in spirit, the spiritually blind and those oppressed in a variety of ways. We must not limit the Lord's words here; millions of believers can bear testimony to some spiritual benefit of these gracious promises.

"The Lord has anointed Me to preach the Gospel to the poor." This was initially the Gospel of the Kingdom. We shall look later at the distinction between that and the Gospel of Grace. Does this mean poor in worldly possessions or poor in spirit? Perhaps both, inasmuch as we find that they often coincide (Mk 10.25). Jesus was not excluding the scribes and Pharisees, but most of them excluded themselves through being haughty in spirit, self righteous and therefore beyond the reach of the Gospel. "They bind heavy burdens, hard to bear, and lay them on men's shoulders; but they themselves will not move them..." (Matt 23.4).

"He has sent Me to heal the brokenhearted." Now this statement is missing from the NU manuscript, so some versions have omitted it. However the fact that it is in other texts, and in the Isaiah passage which Jesus was reading, encourages us to include it. After all, this ministry is surely not limited to any generation or even dispensation. So much that Jesus was about to do in healing diseases, comforting the bereaved, raising the dead to life, restoring loved ones whole and forgiving sins did indeed heal the brokenhearted. Even today that ministry goes on.

 "To preach deliverance to the captives." Now the language here and that of the Isaiah text suggests that Jesus had the Year of Jubilee in mind. For centuries the requirement to release all Jewish citizens from bondage had been largely ignored. There are debates about exact dates, but the year 26/27 AD seems to have been the year of Jubilee, and that could well have been the date of the start of Jesus' public ministry. The year of Jubilee was very much associated with salvation as well as freedom. Perhaps this encouraged the speculation that Jesus might rid the Land of its Roman occupiers. But of course He had no such political agenda.

"And recovery of sight to the blind." Now this is interesting, because Jesus was not quoting from the Isaiah 61 passage. He inserted these words. How many of us, when reading the Bible publicly, pause and add some remark? Hopefully we never do this without saying it in such a way that it is clear to the hearers that it is not part of the text. We may well wonder whether Jesus did the same here. On the other hand, He did have the divine right to add, or to slip in those words from Isa 35.5 without comment. What we can be sure of is that He was indeed about to restore the sight of many blind people within the next three years. Israel's continued spiritual blindness was to be self-induced (Matt 13.15).

"To set at liberty those who are oppressed." Jesus' first miracle recorded by Luke, following His departure from Nazareth, was to exorcise the demon from the possessed Capernaum man. Jesus released many such possessed people during His ministry. So exorcism seems to be one legitimate interpretation. Matthew Henry's comments are slightly different: "Whereas by the guilt of sin we are bound over to the justice of God, sold for sin, Christ lets us know that He has made satisfaction to divine justice for that debt, that His satisfaction is accepted...And whereas, by the dominion of sin in us, we are bound under the power of Satan, Christ lets us know that He has conquered Satan and provided for us grace sufficient to enable us to shake off the yoke". This seems to carry the Acceptable Year into the Church Age.

"To preach the acceptable year of the Lord". Now here we must ask three questions:

- What did Jesus mean by the Acceptable Year of the Lord?
- When did this Acceptable Year begin?
- When did it or will it end?

The three answers are virtually inseparable, but at least we can approach them in this order; we partially answered the second at the start of this chapter.

WHAT IS THE ACCEPTABLE YEAR OF THE LORD?

We are soon going to have to face up to that all important question of whether the Acceptable Year was (a) exclusively for the Jews of Jesus' generation, (b) for the Church Age, (c) for both, (d) for some other grouping or arrangement. We must keep these questions at the back of our minds as we look at the semantics.

The Hebrew word in Isa 61.2 translated 'acceptable' is *ratson*. In the AV it has other English renderings such as 'delight', 'good pleasure' and 'accepted' and, most commonly of all, 'favour'. However 'acceptable' seems to be entirely appropriate, provided that we bear in mind that is to God, to whom it is acceptable rather than to man. It is God's prerogative to accept or look upon favourably.

Even in the sense of an accepted or acceptable time, it is not always necessary to identify it with the particular time which Isaiah said the Messiah was to inaugurate. There may be acceptable times for various activities. We find this in Ps 30.5, "His anger is but for a moment, His favour is for life". David, in distress, cries out to God, "But as for me, my prayer is to You, O Lord, in the acceptable time" (Ps 69.13).

In Isa 49.8 we read: "Thus says the Lord: 'In an acceptable time I have heard You', and in the day of salvation I have helped You'." This is one of those Isaiah passages where the role of servant alternates between the nation and the Messiah, but here it clearly applies to the Messiah; the capital 'Y' of the NKJV for 'You' is entirely appropriate. This is reminiscent of that great Messianic 22nd Psalm where the cry of the Crucified One is at first not heard (vv.1-2) and then heard, "You have answered Me", (v.21). He was not heard when He was made sin for us; but when He had completed His work, it was for the Father an acceptable time to hear His Son.

The Greek word in Lk 4.19 translated 'acceptable' is *dekton*. Its only other AV rendering is 'accepted'. We find it in the same chapter at v.24; "No prophet is accepted in his own country". Peter in his encounter with Cornelius uses it in Acts 10.35: "In every nation whoever fears Him and works righteousness is accepted by Him." In II Cor 6.1-2 Paul writes: "We plead with you not to receive the grace of God in vain. For He says: 'In an acceptable time I have heard you, and in the day of salvation I have helped you.' Behold, now is the accepted time; now is the day of salvation." Words which were initially applied to Christ are now applied to us, inasmuch as we are 'accepted in the Beloved'. What is significant here is the fact that Paul was applying the term well into the Church Age.

Then "**He closed the book** (rolled up the scroll), **and gave it back to the attendant and sat down.**" Ellicott notes: "The chair near the place from which the lesson was read was the pulpit of the Rabbi and to sit down in that chair (as in Matt 23.2) was an assumption by our Lord, apparently for the first time in that synagogue, of the preacher's function." The Matthew reference is to Jesus' talking about the scribes and Pharisees occupying Moses' seat.

Dramatic indeed was this event. "**Today this Scripture is fulfilled in your hearing.**" Here was an authority and challenge which they could not possibly ignore – ultimately they had either to accept or reject it. In the event, they did not even take time to discuss the matter. They led Him to the brow of a nearby hill and would have thrown Him over (v.29). Whatever else we read or do not read into Jesus' announcement, we can hardly dispute the fact that something new and significant was now starting; something unprecedented was about to take place; a new relationship with God was now on offer. Some were profoundly unhappy with it. What changes?

WHEN DID THE ACCEPTABLE YEAR OF THE LORD BEGIN?

We have more or less answered this question already, but may pause on it a little longer, "Today", said Jesus. He cut short Isaiah's prophecy at this most significant juncture. Isaiah went on to add, "and the Day of Vengeance of our God". Jesus did not even comment on that. He did not say that it had been cancelled or that it would never happen. He simply stopped short of reading it. He did not include it in the Scripture which was fulfilled that day. Obviously we will be returning to this unread statement later, as it is the theme of this book, and He certainly did talk about future days of vengeance in His Olivet Discourse (Lk 21.22). What was included in 'fulfilled today' was the start of The Acceptable Year of the Lord. It had now been inaugurated formally for those who had heard it – and they were representative Jews.

THE INITIAL REACTION

Jesus had set forth His immediate programme and was about to demonstrate His credentials. He was not going to do this in the kind of way which Satan had advocated, such as throwing Himself from the pinnacle of the temple and allowing angels to bear Him safely down. (Lk 4.9). This would have negated, for those who witnessed it, the necessity of faith for salvation; it would have bypassed the way of the Cross. One day He will return in spectacular fashion, with the angels following rather than assisting. In that day Satan will not be the prompter but rather the victim. Jesus' challenge was initially going to be a spiritual one, but supported by ample tangible evidence for those who were willing to believe.

Later, when John the Baptist was in prison, evidently puzzled by the turn of events, "he sent two of his disciples and said to Him, 'Are You the Coming One, or do we look for another?' Jesus answered and said to them, 'Go and tell John the things which you hear and see: the blind receive their sight and the lame walk; the lepers are cleansed and the deaf hear; the dead are raised up and the poor have the gospel preached to them'." Jesus was quoting excerpts from Isaiah, from 29.18-19; 35.4-6 and 61.1. John had to be reminded of these confirmatory prophecies. Yes, the evidence was there for all who were prepared to see it; but so was the need for saving faith – that which, if lacking, will ultimately condemn (Jn 3.18).

The miracles which Jesus performed fulfilled the terms of reference which He had declared in the Nazareth synagogue. They were samples of what the prophets had foretold, and which will happen on a world-wide scale in His future Messianic Kingdom. But He was demonstrating there and then that He had both the power and the authority. He was beyond dispute the Messiah of Israel. What were unpopular were His accompanying spiritual demands, which started with the repentance, which His forerunner, John, had already been preaching with mixed reception.

John had been accompanied by a deputation of Pharisees and Sadducees. These are not to be considered as followers or admirers. As spiritual leaders of the nation they were monitoring His ministry. This was a perfectly legitimate and indeed responsible role. Unfortunately they thought of themselves as being above and immune from John's call for repentance. John did not mince his words: "Brood of vipers!...Bear fruits worthy of repentance" (Matt 3.7-8).

When Jesus began His ministry, He attracted a similar group of what in today's terminology we might describe as 'external verifiers'. They represented the nation, and were thus held accountable by God. They were constantly bickering over finer points of ritual which had developed over the centuries. They were particularly censorious over Jesus' custom of doing good on the Sabbath. But in due course there followed certain sad incidents which marked the beginning of the end of The Acceptable Year of the Lord as it applied to the nation.

A mute demoniac was brought to Jesus (Matt 9.32). Priests were sometimes able to cast out demons through the authority invested in them by the Levitical Law. But the demon had to be challenged first verbally, and this could not be done with a mute person. It was considered to be a special Messianic miracle – one which only the Messiah would be able to perform. The same was true of healing a person blind from birth and cleansing a leper (only Naaman, a Gentile, had hitherto been healed of leprosy). Jesus did all of these things. The authenticating evidence was mounting. "But the Pharisees said, 'He casts out demons by the ruler of the demons' " (Matt 9.34). This was a horrendous and suicidal accusation.

In Matt 12.22 *et seq* we read how He healed a demoniac who was both blind and mute. "But when the Pharisees heard it they said, 'This fellow does not cast out demons except by Beelzebub, the ruler of the demons'." It was following this that Jesus gave the stern warning of sinning against the Holy Spirit, by attributing His works to the Devil. This amounted to blasphemy of a type which was unforgivable.

In Lk 11, when similar Beelzebub accusations were made (vv 15-19), Jesus' warning was severe indeed: "The men of Nineveh will rise up in the judgment with this generation and condemn it, for they repented at the preaching of Jonah; and indeed a greater than Jonah is here" (v.32).

FURTHER REACTIONS

Thereafter things changed markedly. In Matt 13.3 we are told that Jesus spoke many things to the multitudes in parables. "The disciples came and asked Him, 'Why do You speak to them in parables?' He answered and said to them, 'because it has been given to you to know the mysteries of the kingdom of heaven, but to them it has not been given'." He went on to quote from Isaiah 6. Observe that several of these Kingdom in Mystery parables of Matthew 13 not only summarise various aspects of the Church Age, but anticipate its ending. The Bible nowhere teaches an endless Christian age from which individuals are removed only at death; such an idea has crept in from the hopeless endless cycle of Oriental religions.

"Matthew 13 is the great chapter which indicates the course of the Kingdom of Heaven in mystery" (AJ Pollock, Things Which Must Shortly Come to Pass). Pollock then goes on to point out that all but one of the parables start with the words "The Kingdom of God is likened". That first one concerns the sower, whose sowing produces the seed of the Kingdom. Writing in Prophetic Witness, Stephen Boreland says: "These parables give a comprehensive view of conditions on the earth in relation to the kingdom programme during the King's absence. This is the classical dispensational view and the only view that takes into account fully the context of these parables in Matthew's gospel."

It is extraordinary how many public readers never proceed beyond the words in Isa 6.8, "Here am I! Send me". Isaiah in fact continues: "And He said: 'Go and tell this people: Keep on hearing, but do not understand; keep on seeing, but do not perceive. Make the heart of this people dull, and their ears heavy and shut their eyes; lest they should see with their eyes, and hear with their ears, and understand with their hearts, and return and be healed'" (Isa 6.9-10).

Isaiah then asked: "Lord, how long?" The answer he received was: "Until the cities are laid waste and without inhabitant, the houses are without a man, the land is utterly desolate, the Lord has removed men far away." (vv.11-12). This was not true of the Old Testament captivities, when people were left to till the land; the Assyrian captivity of the Northern Kingdom had already taken place at the time of Isaiah's writing. So, although Jesus temporarily offered respite from blindness, the reference was clearly to the later 70 AD dispersal. Paul reaffirmed in the closing verses of Acts the continuing blindness of Israel as the Church Age proceeded.

Isaiah's prophecy about blindness is quoted in full or part six times in the New Testament. It must be significant. It seems a strange thing for God to have said, until we pause and consider how wayward the nation was at the time of Isaiah's writing and how longsuffering He had been with them. God reserves the right to say to nations, to congregations and even to individuals: "So far and no further!"

Jesus had come to open hearts, ears and eyes; but there was stubborn resistance at national level, and by the majority at individual level. So the proclamation made through Isaiah was again invoked. We know from the Gospel accounts that the way was never closed for individuals (for the 'whomsoever'), and many from the outset did indeed repent and turn to Him in faith; but they remained a minority. We could trace our way through many events which mark the continual spiritual resistance throughout Jesus' ministry. However we will pause next at Matthew 23, where Jesus delivered the most frightening series of woes to the scribes and Pharisees, in a ministry which had started with conditional blessings or beatitudes. He closed with the words: "See! Your house is left unto you desolate; for I say to you, you shall see Me no more until you say 'Blessed is He who comes in the name of the Lord!'" (vv.38-39).

Any reader who thinks that our line of argument is leading towards a Replacement Theology position should note that crucial "until". Israel has yet to face her blackest hour, but we have abundant evidence that that condition of "until" will one day be met. Without it there can be no "Year of the Lord's Redeemed".

Thereafter we find, in response to Pilate's "Behold your King!", the representative national leaders crying "Away with Him! Crucify Him!...We have no king but Caesar!". (Jn 19.14-15). John summarised this in his prologue: "He came to His own and His own did not receive Him" (Jn 1.11). So we must ask ourselves whether the Acceptable Year of the Lord, ended when they consigned Him to a Roman cross.

THE ACCEPTABLE YEAR AFTER CALVARY

Surely for the nation it ended there and then. There is in effect a national spiritual vacuum until the future prophesied revival of Israel: "Whom the heavens must receive until the restoration of all things, which God has spoken by the mouth of all His holy prophets" (Acts 3.21). But did the Acceptable Year of the Lord end altogether? We can say emphatically that it did not. Let us finish John's quote in the previous paragraph: "But as many as received Him, to them He gave the right to become children of God, even to those who believe in His name." Very well, it might be argued here that John was referring only to individual Jews, who are certainly included. But very soon we see Gentiles being offered the same terms. Gentiles were about to be offered what the Jews had chosen to refuse – the Acceptable Year.

There was however a gracious interim period of about forty years for individual Jews, beginning at Pentecost and ending with the sack of Jerusalem in AD 70; thousands took advantage and believed, but they were invariably castigated, if not persecuted, by the national religious leaders. Jesus told the Eleven that they should be His witnesses in Jerusalem, Samaria and to the ends of the earth, in that sequence (Acts 1.8). "Repentance and remission of sins should be preached in His name to all nations, beginning at Jerusalem." (Lk 24.47). The Gospel was still to be offered in Jerusalem for a limited period. Moreover the Jews dispersed over the empire since, in many cases, Assyrian times, also needed to hear the Gospel. To God a Jew in Baghdad, Glasgow, Moscow or New York is as much a Jew as one in Tel-Aviv. So it was in the days of the early Church.

God's timing was perfect. Multitudes of Jewish pilgrims were in Jerusalem from all over the Roman Empire and elsewhere that Passover and Pentecost. The variety of languages heard on the day that the Holy Spirit came bears testimony to this (Acts 2.8-11). Initially Jerusalem was the world centre of evangelism. Later it was replaced by Antioch. Algernon Pollock writes: "Jerusalem was set aside, and from a Gentile city these servants of God are sent forth. And where did they go? Their divine Master was sent to 'the lost sheep of the house of Israel'. But was the scope of His death limited to the Jews? No; we read: 'The Father sent the Son to be the Saviour of the world' (I Jn 4.14)." (AJ Pollock, Things Which Must Shortly Come to Pass).There had never been a more opportune time in human history. God foreknew it all. Every convert in Judea became a potential missionary after the diaspora.

We have seen how Jesus presented His credentials and how He demonstrated them in practice. He rode into Jerusalem exactly as Zechariah had prophesied (9.9).He did not invite rejection, He literally wept over Jerusalem: "Now as He drew near, He saw the city and wept over it, saying 'If you had known, even you, especially in this your day, the things that make for your peace! But now they are hidden from your eyes...'". He then listed coming calamities and added, "because you did not know the time of your visitation" (Lk 19.41-44). Matthew records Jesus' words to the city: "How often I wanted to gather your children together, as a hen gathers her chicks under her wings, but you were not willing!" (23.37).

We know what the result has been for the Jewish nation. Their capital city was sacked by the Romans. The long list of provisional prophecies of judgment, commencing at Deut 28.16 was fulfilled. "But it shall come to pass if you do not obey the voice of the Lord your God...that all these curses will come upon you and overtake you." This had happened before with the Assyrian and Babylonian captivities. The duration would now be much longer. The Times of the Gentiles, which started in Nebuchadnezzar's time, have been extended until the Lord's return (Lk 21.24 etc).

Within a few centuries Christians had jumped on the bandwagon of the persecutors of the Jews, turning against the olive tree into which they had been grafted. (Rom 11.17). The Spanish Inquisition, the Pogroms and the Holocaust were all perpetrated by people having the audacity to call themselves Christian. It is rather like Judas Iscariot justifying himself by saying that the betrayal had to happen. "Woe to that man by whom He is betrayed", was Jesus' commentary (Lk 22.22). Such is God's attitude to all who practise anti-Semitism. They are personally answerable to God. Those who call themselves evangelical, and yet believe that God has no future purpose for the Jews, not only ignore the powerful testimony of Romans 11, but also ignore the gracious words in Deuteronomy 30 which follow the curses, and discount innumerable predictions of the Prophets. They may not be actively anti-Semitic, but they distort important truths and have an unscriptural perspective of current events.

In the meantime, however, the Church Age progresses. The Church is the ekklesia or called out body. James, referring to an event some time earlier, said, "Simon (Peter) has declared how God at the first visited the Gentiles to take out of them a people for His name" (Acts 15.14). The saved Jew is a minority member, made one with us in Christ – "He (Christ) has broken down the middle wall of division between us" (Eph 2.14). Let none dare ban the evangelisation of the Jews to appease public opinion.

Thus the Acceptable Year of the Lord has been extended to all peoples. One cannot say to 'all nations' inasmuch as the appeal is entirely to individuals within those nations. Certainly God has blessed some nations more than others, but with none other than Israel has He ever entered into a covenant relationship. Addressing a Gentile audience in Athens, Paul said: "The times of ignorance God overlooked, but now commands all men everywhere to repent" (Acts 17.30). This is the continuing Acceptable Year.

In his closing words, Paul, now in Rome, said to a Jewish audience: "The Holy Spirit spoke rightly through Isaiah to our fathers, saying..." (and here he quotes at length from the Isaiah 6 passage about blindness) "Therefore let it be known to you that the salvation of God has been sent to the Gentiles, and they will hear it" (Acts 28.26-28). The Gospel is still preached to the Gentiles; some still hear it; the Acceptable Year of the Lord has yet to end. It is to the mainly Gentile Church at Corinth that Paul wrote in II Cor 6.2, quoting and applying Isa 49.8, "In an acceptable time I have heard you, and in the day of salvation I have helped you."

PROPHECY IN THE CHURCH AGE
The Old Testament prophecies concentrate largely on certain intense periods of fulfilment, such as the Assyrian and Babylonian captivities,

the life and death of the Messiah and the future Day of Vengeance and Year of the Lord's Redeemed. But there were also comparative prophetic vacuums, both in utterance and fulfilment. The Church age, once well under way, has been in such a vacuum.

In a way Jesus has given the Church a commission and told us to get on with it, while promising His presence and authority, empowering us with His Holy Spirit, furnishing us with the complete Bible and giving us a variety of important injunctions. We think of the most frequently quoted Matt 28.19, "Go therefore and make disciples of all nations…", or of Lk 24.47, "that repentance and remission of sins should be preached in His name to all nations, beginning at Jerusalem…", or "You shall receive power…and you shall be witnesses to Me in Jerusalem, and in all Judea and Samaria and to the end of the earth" (Acts 1.8). There is not even a hint that they would ever succeed in the sense that the whole world would be 'Christianised', as some teach. Jesus Himself did not win the hearts of all who heard Him, so who are we to expect such results? But Jesus never failed to seek to win hearts and minds despite this; neither must we.

But what more specific prophecies are there if any? The AD 70 sack of Jerusalem was thoroughly warned against, though for Jews rather than Gentiles. Also there were in Revelation chapters 2 and 3 warnings of coming intense persecution for some of the seven congregations addressed. But otherwise most of the applied prophecies have been in the form of the double or multiple fulfilments which we referred to in our first chapter. Most of these do not truly mature until the Day of Vengeance. People called Historicists, who try to find the entire course of history mapped out in mysterious codes or in Daniel's seventy 'weeks' (about which we have more to say), require a wealth of obscure historical knowledge, and are almost invariably at loggerheads with one another, often by many centuries. Only the relevant Signs of the Times, which point to the impending end of the age, are of great significance to us now.

WHEN WILL THE ACCEPTABLE YEAR OF THE LORD END?
It must be clearly understood that the end of the Acceptable Year of the Lord will not close the door to people being saved, any more than it was impossible for people to be made right with God before it started. Consider the so called 'roll call of faith' in Hebrews 11, which goes back

as far as Abel. But the Acceptable Year of the Lord is the ideal and most beneficial time, and is indeed the only time in which those saved can be included in the Bride of Christ – the Church. No other group in human history has or will have such a privileged relationship to the One who is central in all prophecy.

The end of the Acceptable Year therefore marks the end of the Age in which people may be admitted to the Church, and that means the end of the Church Age. How will it end? It will end by Jesus calling His Church home.

There are some strange concepts about the prophesied Coming Again of the Lord Jesus Christ. Some say He comes at the death of each individual, some say He comes at Communion or The Lord's Supper, while yet others claim that He came in AD 70 at the destruction of Jerusalem. All three are utterly at variance with those dramatic scriptures which describe the Lord's formal return, which we will quote in Chapter 6, though of course we do not deny our Lord's unseen presence at these and other special times.

On the Monday before His crucifixion Jesus had given His lengthy Olivet Discourse concerning the future in answer to a three part question (Matt 24.30, Mk 13.4) concerning the timing of (1) the sack of the Jerusalem, (3) His coming and (3) the end of the age. We must look at this in some detail in our fourth chapter as there is much here about the Day of Vengeance.

But on the night of His betrayal, in the privacy of the upper room, we find Jesus giving a very different prophecy, a promise of reassurance and comfort rather than of warning - despite having other overwhelming things on His mind at this traumatic juncture. "Let not your heart be troubled." What amazing love and tenderness!

The fact that He took time to give such a clear simple promise at this point cannot be overlooked. God forbid that we should ignore or trivialise it! It did not have to be detailed; the disciples had quite enough to cope with in the ensuing hours. The bulk of the details were to be supplied later through Paul. Jesus waited until Judas Iscariot had left the room. The promise concerned only believers. "In My Father's house are many dwellings...I go to prepare a place for you. And if I go and prepare a place for you, I will come again and receive you to Myself, that where I am there you may be also" (Jn 14.1-3).

He prefaced this with the injunction that they should accept these words as being as trustworthy, coming from Him as from the Father, in Whom they believed implicitly. We, with the benefit of hindsight, have no difficult in accepting this; but they were about to see their Lord arrested, endure two farcical trials and be summarily crucified. They needed this special endorsement: "Ye believe in God, believe also in Me".

He said that He was going to prepare many dwelling places. These dwelling places are elsewhere, in the place for which He was soon to be seen to be departing (Acts 1.9), in other words in His Father's House in Heaven. This promised coming is to be FOR HIS OWN.

We have seen, therefore, that it was a necessary and timely promise. It was also an unambiguous one, even though it was not elaborated. People whose theories it does not fit prefer to ignore it. There are no linguistic excuses for distorting these words. How much confusion could be avoided if only the words were taken seriously. The comfort is still there for those who might otherwise fear the worst from the end of this age. The promise was also an obvious one, because Jesus added, "If it were not so, I would have told you". Isn't that gloriously reassuring?

Some teach that Jesus is coming only once, meeting resurrected believers half way and then proceeding to earth to accomplish all those many great tasks which are to bring to an end the Day of Vengeance before the year of the Lord's Redeemed. We seem to be faced with a pair of alternatives, as if Jesus were implying either:-

a. "I am about to leave you and prepare a place for you. One day I will return for you, meeting you midway, then we'll go back to My place." Or:-

b. "I am about to leave you and prepare a place for you. One day I will return to you, meeting you midway, then we'll go back to your place."

Which do you believe? Both cannot be true. We cannot sit on the fence. Jesus said that He would receive us unto Himself, not that we would receive Him unto ourselves. As Paul says, and we hear his words re-echoed in many other Scriptures, our hope is laid up in Heaven (Col 1.5), not on earth.

We choose option (a). Thus we re-affirm that when He comes FOR His Church the Acceptable Year will end and the Day of Vengeance of our God will begin on earth and, as we shall see later, that when He comes TO, the Day of Vengeance will end and the Day of the Lord's Redeemed will be inaugurated. Option (b) would mean that those who sleep in Christ would never be in their resurrection bodies in the place Jesus has gone to prepare until after the Millennium, and that living raptured believers would not see it at all for a thousand years!

A common and understandable concern of parents regarding the Rapture is the fate of their potentially abandoned babies or children. Will they be left to undergo the Tribulation alone? We do not believe so, though we have very little direct teaching to pass on. Surely we can trust the Lord, who said "Take heed that you do not despise one of these little ones, for I say to you that in heaven their angels always see the face of My Father who is in heaven" (Matt 18.10). This is a unique verse, but reassuring. We believe that they will somehow be taken too, though not, we feel as part of the Church (a few would disagree), because they have not come to Christ in the same way as the rest of us. Naturally, irrespective of their age, they will need to be redeemed by the blood of the Lamb too. David wrote: "Behold, I was brought forth in iniquity, and in sin my mother conceived me" (Ps 51.5). This applies to everyone except the Lord Jesus Himself, who was conceived sinlessly of the Holy Spirit. We do not know how or when the precious blood will be applied.

There seem to be unaccounted people in Heaven, for instance in Revelation 5, who may perhaps include the still-born or those who have never reached the age of discretion. This concern, which many of us who are or have been parents have shared, should not discourage us from looking forward to the Lord's return. Surely there would have been a warning to this effect somewhere in Scripture. Jesus' words about the pregnant and nursing mothers in Matt 24.19 are about a different scenario. It may be that God has not revealed more about these matters in order to prevent parents in crisis situations from slaying their infants in order to ensure their salvation. We feel that God makes similar provision for the profoundly mentally handicapped, though not necessarily with regard to the Rapture. We must leave these difficult matters in His safe hands.

HOW WILL THE ACCEPTABLE YEAR OF THE LORD END?
While there is much wonderful information about our translation into resurrection bodies in I Cor 15.35-44, the key verses elaborating Jesus' promise to His apostles are in I Thessalonians 4, where Paul declares a 'mystery', in other words something quite new to his readers. They were written as words of comfort to young believers worried about their departed loved ones, and should be of even greater comfort to us as the time draws near.

"But I do not want you to be ignorant, brethren, concerning those who have fallen asleep, lest you sorrow as others who have no hope. For if we believe that Jesus died and rose again, even so God will bring with Him those who sleep in Jesus. For this we say to you by the word of the Lord, that we who are alive and remain until the coming of the Lord will by no means precede those who are asleep. For the Lord Himself shall descend from heaven with a shout, with the voice of an archangel, and with the trumpet of God. And the dead in Christ shall rise first. Then we who are alive and remain shall be caught up together with them in the clouds to meet the Lord in the air. And thus we shall always be with the Lord. Therefore comfort one another with these words" (I Thess 4.13-17).

From the time of Joseph Mede in the 17th Century this became known as the Rapture, a word derived from the perfectly good Latin rendering *raptare* in v.17 of the Vulgate translation of the original Greek *harpazo*. The prevalent claim that this was a 19th Century invention is nonsense. People are entitled not to use this particular word if they do not like it; but they are emphatically not entitled to question the promise of the catching up of believers, both dead and alive. If they must doubt God's promises, they are not entitled to encourage others to doubt.

Paul has been given the immense privilege of disclosing to us this hitherto secret element in God's plan for the ages. It explains Jesus' promise in John 14.1-3 as no other passage does. It is remarkably simple and unambiguous, though it throws up immense problems for those whose faith cannot cope with the fact that God can indeed accomplish what must be just about be the greatest miracle since Creation. And it could well happen within our lifetime! In the simplest possible terms it tells us that God is going to take His redeemed home; moreover it tells us how. What it does not tell us is when, though we do have important signs.

We are going now to examine the implications of the I Thessalonians 4 passage. Many scriptures confirm that when the believer dies he or she goes immediately into the Lord's presence and a state of consciousness, joy and blessing, while the body decays. Here we are reminded that the bodies remain in the grave until one future glorious day, when the "dead in Christ shall rise first". This is the main harvest of which the Lord Himself was the Firstfruits – "Christ the firstfruits, afterward those that are Christ's at His coming" (I Cor 15.23). The gleanings we will encounter later. These three harvest stages come from Leviticus 23 and were endorsed by God.

This dispels any idea of Mary, Peter and a variety of other 'saints' risen and employed in special capacities in Heaven. This is an adaptation of ancient heathenism. All believers are described as saints in the NT. When Constantine publicly embraced Christianity on behalf of the Roman Empire, many spiritual compromises were made to preserve the popular parts of polytheistic heathenism. Roman and Greek gods became identified with Christian heroes. Demeter, Aphrodite or Hera became Mary, introducing into apostate Christianity a 'Queen of Heaven' (see Jer 7.18 and 44.17 *et seq* for God's exceedingly stern view of such a title). From there it was a short step to having a 'Mother of God', a concept going back to Nimrod, and classed in Ezek 8.14 as an abomination. What a travesty that that blessed woman, who acknowledged "God my Saviour" (Lk 1.47), should have been accorded such associations down through the centuries! The Father shares His glory only with His Son (Jn 17.5).

If these are still in their graves, who are people invoking when they pray to them, rather than to God, to whom all prayer should be made in Jesus' name, the ONLY acceptable one and the New Testament pattern? We are not being pedantic. But many sincere people are being deeply misled and honour is being diverted from Jesus to somebody who cannot be Mary or other 'saints', who, as we know, are not yet in a position to receive it even if they wanted to. They would no doubt react with horror, as did the angel before whom an overwhelmed John fell down to worship; "See that you do not do that...Worship God" (Rev 22.9).

When Jesus comes FOR us, He will bring with Him the souls and spirits of the dead in Christ to meet their new bodies. The meeting is said to take place in the air, in other words within this creation, where their bodies have lain and whence they must be raised incorruptible. The human trinity of body, soul and spirit, broken by death, will be restored. Immediately afterwards "we who are alive and remain shall be caught up together with them in the clouds to meet the Lord in the air" (I Thess 4.17). "We also eagerly wait for the Saviour, the Lord Jesus Christ, who will transform our lowly body that it may be conformed to His glorious body" (Phil 3.20-21). We cannot go to Heaven in these corruptible bodies, even if we wanted to (I Cor 15.50). That is why both the meeting and the transformation must take place somewhere within our own atmosphere, sometimes known as the first heaven. From there Jesus Christ, the Church's Bridegroom, will take us home to His Father's house, where He has been busy preparing for us.

Some respected commentators believe that the mention of Jesus descending in I Thess 4.16 is a parenthetical reference to His later Coming in Power; others believe that it refers to His coming to the air for His saints. As He will be descending on both occasions, it is not a serious bone of contention.

If we believe that God is faithful and able to keep His promises, we will have no difficulty in believing this stupendous miracle by the One who designed DNA and who called the worlds into being. Note well that there is here no mention in I Thess 4 of His intervention at the Battle of Armageddon, no disposal of Satan, the Beast or False Prophet, no judgment of the sheep and goats, no divine touch down at the Mount of Olives. Neither is there any mention of the resurrection of the unsaved. Why? Simply because on this earlier occasion He is coming FOR and not coming TO. The other events are guaranteed to happen at their appropriate times – but not at this time.

DEVIATIONS AND MISUNDERSTANDINGS
God is omniscient. He knew that when Jesus first offered Himself to His own nation, as the Messiah whom they claimed to be awaiting, He would be rejected. Similarly He had known beforehand that the Fall would

occur when He created man and He had already planned for Calvary. This helps us to understand the phrase, "Whose names have not been written in the Book of Life of the Lamb slain from the foundation of the world" (Rev 13.8). God foreknew those who would accept and those who would reject salvation.

Thus the accusations levelled at Pre-Millennialists that they believe that the Church Age was an afterthought is sheer calumny. I quote from my own article published in Your Tomorrow in August 1996. "The first is an article by the late Loraine Boettner, which is still in circulation and being quoted, entitled 'The Fatal Error of Pre-Millennialism'. The opening paragraph reads: 'Pre-Millennialism holds that Christ at His First Advent came to establish a Kingdom, that He so offered Himself to His people the Jews, but that when they rejected Him and crucified Him He postponed the Kingdom and established the Church as a temporary alternative and substitute, and that this was not foreseen by the Old Testament prophets nor mentioned in the Old Testament.' As a travesty of the truth it certainly takes a lot of beating, doesn't it? The 'Fatal Error' is in Dr Boettner's understanding of Pre-Millennialism."

The danger in the above is that a little powerful untruth is mixed with a good deal of truth. The accusation that Pre-Millennialists think of the Church Age as "a temporary alternative and substitute" on God's part is an appalling distortion of what others believe. We believe that it is utterly fundamental to God's plans that Jesus' offer of Himself as Messiah was totally sincere and genuine, even though He fully realised what the outcome would be.

Did Dr Boettner really believe that Pre-Millennialists think that Jesus was putting on an act when He wept over Jerusalem? Those are the implications if one thinks it through. The frightening thing is that a lot of people believe this sort of disinformation. It discourages believers from studying the prophetic word. "All Scripture is given by inspiration of God and is profitable..." (II Tim 3.16). Some would like to insert "except prophecy" into that text!

There is a good deal of confusion about the Church Age and the Kingdom. In our penultimate chapter we will review how all the promises concerning Christ's Kingdom on earth will be fulfilled. The Kingdom in its fullness was not cancelled – it was merely postponed until the Year of the Lord's Redeemed. "The kingdom is in **mystery** now as it will be in **display** when Christ rules as the King of Israel and as the Son of Man over the whole world" (AJ Pollock).

CHAPTER 3

An Overview of The Day of Vengeance

ALL ARE REQUIRED TO REPENT

"Truly, these times of ignorance God overlooked, but now commands all men everywhere to repent, because He has appointed a day on which He will judge the world in righteousness by the Man whom He has ordained. He has given assurance of this to all by raising Him from the dead" (Acts 17.30-31). From start to finish the Acceptable Year of the Lord demands repentance. When it has run its course the Day of Vengeance will follow in the form of judgment of the world. The demand for repentance at that time will apparently be emphasised more than at any other time in history. This period will be quite distinct from the various judgments of individuals.

REACTION TO THE RAPTURE

Throughout the remainder of this book we will sometimes use the term Tribulation Period as an alternative to the Day of Vengeance. It is wrong to call it The Great Tribulation, as this applies only to the second half. Sceptics like to point out that tribulation is said in the New Testament not to be confined to this time, but to be on-going, hence our preference for the Day of Vengeance of our God. The Great Tribulation is accorded a definite article in Rev 7.14; it will be quite unique.

What will be the reaction when, in the twinkling of an eye, millions of Christians simultaneously disappear? Doubtlessly there will be some surprises over those who are taken and those who are left behind; but there will be no mistakes, because the Lord knows those who are His. Will there be mass repentance as a result? Certainly millions will be saved in the period following. However, there is a strong indication in II Thess 2.10-11 that those, who had previously been presented with the Gospel and had either rejected or deliberately postponed a decision, will be unable to repent: "for this reason God will send them strong delusion, that they should believe the lie". We dare not take any gambles when it comes to the redemption of our eternal souls. For every individual who hears the Gospel, "Now is the accepted time; behold now is the day of salvation" (II Cor 6.2).

We may speculate about other matters, but cannot always be sure. Will there be an incredibly large number of accidents, as aircraft pilots, car drivers, motor cyclists and others suddenly vanish from their vehicles? It seems probable, as this could provoke widespread anger against God; but we do not know for certain. God is perfectly capable of preventing such a scenario, and the angels could be kept very busy!

Will there be lots of little piles of left-behind clothing, handbags, wallets, pacemakers, dentures and so on? We simply do not know. Our only clue might be the folded graveclothes in the Lord's empty tomb. Will people see us disappear, in the same way that the disciples saw their Lord taken up until a cloud received Him from their sight? We cannot answer, but suspect that they will not. When Elijah was translated, search parties spent three days hunting for him in case God's Spirit had deposited him elsewhere (II Kings 2.17). The old prophet had been unsure whether even his successor, Elisha, would see him go (v 10); in fact he did, but it is doubtful if anyone else saw the chariot of fire. Many may be glad to see the back of us! Ingenious and even sinister may be the explanations offered for our sudden departure.

We know from the II Thessalonians passage that there is going to be some sort of cunning lie, a strong delusion, something credible to those who want to believe it. One thing is clear. While Satan has his personal programme for this time, the climax to all his scheming since before Eden, God also has His programme. And it is God who is in overall control, and who, just as He did in Job's time, will allow Satan only so much scope. It will be Satan's final opportunity, free from the presence of the Church with its special indwelling of the Holy Spirit, which will apparently cease with the Rapture (see II Thess 2.7). Satan's dreadful fate is assured, and we might well wonder why he persists in his evil ways, and yet we know that hell-bent mortals may equally ruthlessly court disaster. And of course we simply cannot comprehend, and this is perhaps just as well, the awful depravity of that mighty fallen angel, who in eternity past was the anointed covering cherub, "perfect in all your ways" until "…your heart was lifted up" (Ezek 28.15 &17).

This strong delusion may well be his first priority, and it could be the way in which he first brings to prominence his Antichrist, who has such a central part to play in the Day of Vengeance. This is the second person of the trinity of evil, in which the third person is the False Prophet. The first person is Satan himself, also described in Rev 12 as the Devil, the great dragon, that serpent of old and the accuser of the brethren. The Antichrist or false Christ or Messiah is also called the beast (Rev 13.1), the first beast (Rev 13.12), the man of sin, the son of perdition (II Thess 2.3), the little horn (Dan 7.8) and the prince who is to come (Dan 9.26). We will refer to him hereafter simply as the Beast; there have been lesser antichrists. We need to know about him at this juncture because his activities are intimately linked to the duration of the Day of Vengeance. We will discover much more about his roles and his fearful destination later.

There has been much speculation, both wild and considered, about the nationality of this prince. He might be a prince of the apostate church in order to explain his rise to power and influence within the Revived Roman Empire. It is possible that He will be a cosmopolitan Jew in order to qualify him for recognition by Orthodox Jews, however one could argue that it is the False Prophet, who will rise to prominence as his deputy at the mid-point of the seven years, who will be Jewish, or at least partly so. We will learn more about both of these when we look in our next chapter at Revelation 13.

One result of the Rapture will be to deprive the political and commercial world, particularly the formerly 'Christian world', of many key leaders and specialists in various fields. There will be an unprecedented leadership vacuum with an unprecedented malevolent personality ready to fill the void. We can only guess how much impact this will have, but it is difficult not to visualise a variety of grave crises. Crises have in the past given unscrupulously opportunist leaders, such as Adolf Hitler, situations to exploit. Such people often give initially the appearance of being benevolent dictators, and this man will be no exception. The main qualifications of such people tend to be charisma, strength and cunning, rather than integrity and moral qualities. In a world now deprived of the salt of the earth, this will be truer than ever. Satan's own superman is waiting in the wings.

We could speculate endlessly how he will come to the forefront; although when he does he should be clearly recognisable to those conversant with the prophetic word. Only half way through the Day of Vengeance will his true character become apparent to more people. This will be the person who will pull off the world's biggest political coup. He will appear to solve the Israeli-Palestinian impasse. Hitherto the world's most powerful figures have failed signally to do this; and we suggest that they will continue to fail until this Prince-Who-Is-To-Come steps onto the scene. As politicians continue to bluster and blunder and as terrorists persist in causing misery and unrest, God has been steering the world inexorably to this crisis point.

Two and a half thousand years ago God through Zechariah talked of Jerusalem becoming an international burden: "In that day I will make Jerusalem a very heavy stone for all peoples; all who would heave it away will surely be cut in pieces, though all nations of the earth are gathered against it" (12.3). The AV's 'burdensome stone' is most descriptive. Now that verse actually applies to the latter part of the Day of Vengeance, but this international running sore has for decades been near bursting point and is ever becoming more virulent. The Beast will apparently provide a cure, to the wonder and acclamation of the watching world and the deception of many Jews. What is of crucial interest to us here is that his solution will consist of a seven year security treaty which he will either impose or negotiate (Dan 9.27). And these seven years give us a very good idea of the length of the Day of Vengeance. Unless the treaty is signed on the actual day of the Rapture, which seems highly unlikely, we can simply say that it will last seven plus years. Now we must look at the political background to this Antichrist before returning to this momentous but sinister covenant.

THE BACKGROUND OF THE PRINCE THAT IS TO COME
First we must turn to three visions in Daniel, the favourite target book of critics, including many orthodox Jewish rabbis, who feel most uncomfortable with it, because the accuracy of some of it to them inconvenient or condemnatory prophecies is so easily demonstrated. Jesus gave it His seal of approval by quoting from it, so no Christian is entitled to doubt it. The visions are found in chapters 2, 7 and 9. Daniel and Revelation are the only two books in the Bible with special exhortations to preserve them. Both should be treasured by all believers.

After Judah's exile to Babylon and long after the other tribes had been taken to Assyria, God gave a portentous dream to King Nebuchadnezzar, a dream which his renowned magicians and astrologers were unable to recount or interpret. God wanted His man, Daniel, to do this, in order for him to be recognised by the king and to preserve the details for posterity. The dream covered what we know as the Times of the Gentiles, which were to start immediately (around 603 BC) and are to continue to the end of the Day of Vengeance, after which Israel will be restored to world pre-eminence.

The dream described an awesome image with a head of gold, chest of silver, loins and thighs of brass and legs of iron (2.32-35). These stages represented a succession of empires which were to dominate the world around the Promised Land down through the ensuing ages. Jesus confirmed that "Jerusalem will be trampled by the Gentiles until the times of the Gentiles are fulfilled" (Lk 21.24), eloquently confirming that neither the Old Testament nor the events of 70 AD have exhausted the significance of these things.

The gold represented Nebuchadnezzar's own Babylon (v.37), which was to be succeeded by the silver Medo-Persian Empire, which was to be overthrown in turn by bronze Greece, which was eventually to be replaced by iron Rome. The vision in chapter 7 confirms these identities by name, apart from Rome, which was unknown in the Middle East at the time, but whose identification is unmistakable. All this has of course been fulfilled. But then came the feet and toes, obviously an extension of the legs (the Roman Empire), yet treated separately, divided, devalued and mixed with alien, fragile ceramic clay. Nebuchadnezzar perceived a stone "cut out without hands" smash these feet and become a great mountain which filled the whole earth (Dan 2.35). Daniel explained that this stone will become a great, world dominating kingdom which will last forever. "The great God has made known to the king what will come to pass after this. The dream is certain, and its interpretation is sure" (v.45). That should be good enough for us.

Now the mountain cannot be the Church, which, far from destroying the Roman Empire, co-existed with it and its splits and fragments for centuries; and of course the Church's role was never to smash. Moreover there is no reason to believe from the vision that it is, as is sometimes suggested, a 'spiritual' kingdom'. It is another visible kingdom on earth, greater than any of its predecessors. A host of OT prophecies points to this. We have to wait until the New Testament (I Corinthians 15.24) to discover how Jesus will deliver this earthly Kingdom to His Father at the very end of the world.

So this is a vision which takes us from six centuries before the birth of Jesus right up to the future Year of the Lord's Redeemed. The smashing of the feet marks the end of Day of Vengeance. Note that each of these empires has controlled the area, the title of which God has given *in perpetua* to Israel. In the feet we find the first indications of a sort of Revived Roman Empire which will dominate Europe and part of the Middle East immediately before Christ's return in power. We want to know something of the ruler of this final form of empire, the lowest stage of the image – the man with the influence to "solve" the Israeli-Palestinian impasse.

The use of the term 'Palestinian' implies no recognition; we use it only for convenience here. Where in the Authorised Version (KJV) the word 'Palestine' occurs, it should be rendered 'Philistine'. God cast out the original inhabitants of the land because of their sin and He retains the right to dispossess any nation. Palestine and Palestinian are Roman terms. 'Promised Land' is a useful term for what legally extends from the River of Egypt (not the Nile) to the Euphrates. God gave the title to Israel, but tenancy at any time is dependent upon their obedience. Thus it has often been forfeited.

We will for the present pause only briefly at the vision in Daniel 7, one given directly to the prophet rather than to the king. We will skip over the descriptions and sequence of the first three empires, which match the gold, silver and bronze levels, interesting though these are. The fourth beast, equates to the iron section or Rome, and is described as more dreadful than its predecessors (v.19).

From it there eventually arise ten horns or concurrent kings, from among whom there emerges another blasphemous horn, a little horn or upstart (vv.21 & 25), a king or ruler who will persecute the saints and challenge God Himself. His rise to power appears to be disputed briefly, because three kings have to be deposed by him (v.8); however with Satan's backing he prevails. This is the same person, the Beast, who has his power base in the Revived Roman Empire. This conglomerate empire is to be in existence until it is destroyed, when "the kingdom shall be given to the saints" (vv.26-27). While the Roman Empire has continued in some form or other through the centuries, as Byzantium, the Holy Roman Empire and the Roman Catholic Church, it is apparent from Daniel 2 and other visions that its power peaks twice, once in the past and once in the future, almost but not quite to the point of being two separate entities – the legs and feet of its ancient and latter day forms.

We learn about the Beast's empire from Daniel and Revelation. The difficulty with Daniel is that some prophecies have double fulfilments in ancient history and the latter days, and in others we have to identify the cut-off point between the ancient and the future. But following the introductory three chapters of Revelation everything is unquestionably future. Revelation puts much of Daniel in perspective. Thus Rev 17.12 confirms that the ten kings, found both there and in Dan 7.24, who lend their support to the Beast, are to survive until they are to be destroyed by the Lamb at Armageddon.

ISLAMIC INVOLVEMENT?

In our opening chapter we stressed the need for caution in making unqualified statements where identifications are still tenuous. We re-emphasise this caution now, because we will from time to time be discussing the identity of the final Antichrist or Beast and the False Prophet, as well as the constitution of the Beast's empire and the nature of the final manifestation of Mystery Babylon. We have no reason to believe that this empire exists as yet within its final borders, although the ten component nations may well do. There is likely to be massive political reshuffling after the Rapture, with the Beast emerging from obscurity to take the throne of this new power bloc.

For several centuries these have been associated with apostate Rome; this interpretation of relevant prophecies has stood persecuted believers in good stead. Long before the Treaty of Rome was signed, establishing the European Common Market, and before Winston Churchill made any such proposal, students of prophecy were predicting a Rome centred 'United States of Europe' as the feet of iron and clay of Nebuchadnezzar's image and thus the Revived Empire. It was interesting speculation. However ancient Rome made few inroads in terms of settlement beyond the Forth Clyde Valley, the Rhine and the Danube. Community membership now extends as far as Finland and the Baltic States. We must not be too clever in anticipating post-

Rapture details. Has recent history compelled us tentatively to adjust our views?

Fifty years ago, as a young acting platoon sergeant in the western fringe of Abu Dhabi in what was then the Trucial Oman, I took turns with my platoon commander watch keeping at night; of course we had sentries. I had a kerosene lamp and had plenty of time to read. My parents had just sent me a copy of Geoffrey King's commentary on Daniel. I must have gone through it carefully three times, and was duly impressed. I accepted most of what he wrote, as I still do.

He felt that because the empires represented by the upper four stages of Nebuchadnezzar's image had all in turn occupied the Holy Land, the Islamic nations which had occupied it for many centuries must be the feet of iron and clay (Islam considers itself to be a nation). He questioned the idea of a Revived Roman Empire. Having referred to the preoccupation of NATO and Warsaw Pact countries with one another, he wrote: "You wait and see, when all the rest of the world is endeavouring to get itself ready, building itself up, you wait and see; out of the Mohammedan world will rise a great figure who will conquer the world and turn out to be this very man of sin". We need not go into the details; it is well argued. Later he adds: "That is the last dictator of the world before Jesus comes. Hypnotic eyes, mesmeric eloquence, - well, Hitler all over again, only much worse. As I've said before, watch 'the Moslem Belt' today!" (Daniel, A Detailed Description).

However there are problems with his interpretation too, including the fact that during the Tribulation period a number of carefully identified Muslim nations, notably Libya, Egypt and Syria, once part of the ancient Roman Empire, are shown to be acting independently of each other and even in conflict with the Beast's empire.

While I was very impressed, I could not help thinking of the poverty-stricken backward land in which we were stationed, with very little revenue and no mains electricity anywhere. There were thirty of us in that location, providing security for hopeful oil prospectors, but no black gold had been struck. Admittedly some Middle Eastern countries were oil-rich even then, and some were well enough equipped for local wars. But nothing was on a potentially global scale. How that has changed in half a century! Mr King's words have a certain appeal to the modern mind.

Now we feel that the truth lies somewhere between, and that neither apostate Christianity nor militant Islam will initially hold the monopoly in the Mediterranean area. Somehow – and it seems unlikely that this will be clear before the Rapture – Islam is certain to play a significant role. The mixture of iron with clay adds to the impression of an unnatural alliance. Later we will consider how a Muslim may fit into the 'trinity of evil'. We will periodically return to these matters as our studies progress through the Day of Vengeance.

THE DURATION OF THE DAY OF VENGEANCE

Before we look at the Beast's role in the timing of this period, we must emphasise that it is not he, but the Lord Jesus Christ, who is to inaugurate the Day of Vengeance. He alone is shown to be worthy (Rev 5.8-9). In that glorious vision given to John and recorded in Revelation 5, the whole of Heaven, including the raptured saints, is to witness the quest for and identification of one worthy to open the seven Seals of the Day of Vengeance. He is worthy because of His Calvary credentials manifested in His visible proof of being "the Lamb as though it had been slain". He is worthy because He voluntarily became a Man, "the Lion of the Tribe of Judah and the Root of David", both Champion and Royal Kinsman of Israel. The ultimate destruction of Israel's enemies will be high on His agenda during the Day of Vengeance, when the Church will be safe in glory. The enemies of God's people of whatever branch are God's enemies.

He it is who opens the first of the seven Seals and allows the rider on the white horse, who is the Beast, the first 'Horseman of the Apocalypse', to go forth (Rev 6.1-2). Suggestions that this rider is Christ Himself are preposterous, despite superficial similarities, when we look at the horrific nature of the other visionary horsemen and when we compare this rider with the Coming Christ of Revelation 19. God is in control throughout, not the Beast or his master. We have much more to say about these Seals later.

Not only does He open the first Seal; He opens all seven. It is the final Seal which lets loose the Trumpet and Bowl judgments. This indeed is the day in which the Father judges the rebellious fallen world by the Man whom He has appointed. The scene in Heaven is one of praise and adoration, which we may at first find difficult to comprehend in view of the judgments about to commence, but, as the late Dr John F

Walvoord writes, "The true occupation of the child of God should be one of praise and worship of the God of glory while awaiting the fulfilment of His prophetic Word" (The Revelation of Jesus Christ).

The third Daniel vision in chapter 9.20-27 is so important that it is personally transmitted to the prophet by one of only two named holy angels in Scripture, Gabriel. Surely the Holy Spirit is emphasising here the importance of this Daniel prophecy by having it delivered by this mighty angel who stands in God's presence (Lk 1.19). Yet some who are entranced by Gabriel's role in the Christmas message have never read or considered this passage, which though not so directly pertinent to the Church, is given a high profile by God and referred to by Jesus.

One should read the whole section; we will give excerpts only now, though we will be returning later. Gabriel gives us a prophetic programme with exact figures. The length of Israel's four hundred years of affliction in Egypt was prophesied precisely (Gen 15.13), as was the forty years extension of the wanderings in the Sinai desert (Num 14.33) and the seventy year Babylonian captivity (Jer 25.11). So we have no grounds whatsoever to doubt the precision either of the statistics we are about to review, or the six times stated thousand years of Revelation 20, one of the chief targets of the mockers.

We find the word 'week' used for a group of seven. The original word can indeed mean week, but can equally apply to any other group of seven. Such groups of seven are associated with the jubilee calculations elsewhere. We will use the better word 'heptad', though unfortunately it is not sufficiently familiar for normal use. The years used in prophecy and found elsewhere in the Old Testament are luni-solar years of 360 days. This may well be the length of the Antediluvian year and of the future Millennial year. We cannot be sure, but huge cosmic changes occurred at the Flood and will occur at the time of the Lord's return in power. It could be that it is our current chronology that is unnatural.

The aged Daniel had been pouring out his exemplary intercessory prayer of confession for his nation, having just ascertained from the scroll of Jeremiah that the seventy year Babylonian exile was near its end (Dan 9.2). Here at least was one godly man believing in and applying predictive prophecy and not doubting God-given statistics. His faith and humility were recognised by God, and he was graciously given by Him a summary of the number of years which were to expire before his nation's ultimate restoration. His desire for a spiritually revived Israel was not to be realised in his lifetime, or indeed for many lifetimes; but it was assured. The restoration soon to be accomplished with the return from Babylon was to be only partial and temporary, both spiritually and politically.

Gabriel announced: "Seventy weeks are determined for your people and your holy city, to finish transgression, to make an end of sins, to make reconciliation for iniquity, to bring in everlasting righteousness, to seal up vision and prophecy, and to anoint the Most Holy" (v.24). The NKJV has appropriately and helpfully inserted an asterisk at 'weeks' leading to a footnote saying "literally sevens, and so throughout the chapter". Thus four hundred and ninety years are determined for Israel and Jerusalem to usher in the listed features, some of which have yet to occur. Elsewhere we have abundant confirmation, as we shall soon see, that the 490 applies specifically to actual years, rather than to any symbolic period.

Then in verse 25 a precise start date for the statistics is provided, a nominated day around a century after the time of the vision. It is a date which can be corroborated from the records of the Medo-Persian Empire, a day in July 445 BC which equates to the first day of the Jewish month Nisan, when Artaxerxes gave the order to build and restore the Jerusalem temple (see v.25). The 490 was then divided into three groups of 49, 434 and 7 respectively. The first group is for us now of historical importance only and concerned the building of the city and wall. At the appropriate time it was of great importance, and confirmed to the devout among the builders that they were on course in God's plans, despite their trials. Such reassurance is one of the best "spin-offs" of the Bible's predictive prophecy.

What is of enormous significance is that the second group, taking us to the end of the 483rd year, has been demonstrated by Sir Robert Anderson, head of London's CID in late Victorian times, and confirmed since by many other authorities, to take us right up to Palm Sunday, as we know it, in Nisan 32 AD, the day on which Jesus presented Himself at Jerusalem for recognition or rejection. Gabriel told Daniel that the 434 years were to be from the rebuilding of the wall "until Messiah the Prince" (v.25). We know how Jesus came in fulfilment of Zechariah's prophecy which we have already quoted: "Behold, your King is coming to you; He is just and having salvation, lowly and riding on a donkey" (Zech 9.9).

As Jesus approached Jerusalem on that fateful Sunday, the crowd of pilgrims shouted out from the words of the Messianic Great Hallel or Praise (Psalms 113 to 118), "Blessed is He who comes in the name of the Lord!" (Matt 21.9 & Lk 19.38). The Pharisees, representing the city, ordered Jesus to rebuke His disciples, which He of course did not do. "Now as He drew near, He saw the city and wept over it, saying, 'If you had known, even you, especially in **this your day**, the things that make for your peace! But now they are hidden from your eyes..... You did not know the time of your visitation'" (Lk 19.41-44). This *was* their day; the very day foretold by the angel hundreds of years before. But they rejected their promised Prince. One day the representatives of the same city will be deceived into accepting an impostor prince, a false Christ. What a price there will be to pay! In the meantime the seventy weeks of years were suspended at this, the 483 year point; they have yet to resume.

But then, according to Gabriel, following this 483rd year "Messiah is to be cut off, but not for Himself" (v.26). Our minds go to that wonderful prophetic picture in Isaiah of the vicarious suffering Saviour bearing our sins (Isa 53.4-5) "not for Himself". Before Daniel was told of the final seven years he was told of the "people of the prince who is to come, (who) shall destroy the city and the sanctuary" (v.26). Well, we know that it was Rome in 70 AD which next destroyed both city and sanctuary; it is significant that Gabriel did not include that event within any of the three groups of years, inasmuch as it was due to occur within the long interval between the latter two.

We pick up the final group of seven in v.27. "He (that is the prince that shall come) shall confirm a covenant with many for one week (seven years); but in the middle of the week he shall bring an end to sacrifice and offering. And on the wing of abominations shall be one who makes desolate" (v.27). The text is not easy. What we have here is a latter day prince of Roman extraction making a seven year treaty, which will allow for Jewish (Levitical) sacrifices in Jerusalem, but which he will break at the midway point, when the Abomination of Desolation, which Jesus Himself confirmed as yet future, will be set up.

Now the obvious question is this: what happens in the interval beyond the precisely determined end of the 483rd year and the start of the final seven? Between Messiah presenting Himself and being cut off by crucifixion lies the entire Church Age, in other words almost the entire Acceptable Year. This is confirmed by the fact that, since the 70 AD destruction of Jerusalem, no covenant has ever been made which permitted the resumption of sacrifices on the Temple Mount. This to neighbouring Anti-Semitic states would be anathema. Admittedly there was some continuation of the sacrifices between 70 and 135 AD on the Temple Mount, but these were never sanctioned by any treaty. In the light of current world affairs only a political master stroke could negotiate or impose such a treaty or covenant.

TWO TIMES THREE-AND-A-HALF

So, following the Rapture of the Church, but not quite coinciding with it, we have a significant seven year period, split into two equal periods of three and a half years. In case our logic seems tenuous, we will check whether we can find elsewhere any mention of either the seven or two lots of three and a half years. We can. We will refer to these individually later, but group them together here in order of appearance with the minimum comment.

- Dan 7.25:- The Beast will blaspheme God and persecute the saints for "a time, times and half a time".
- Dan 9.27:- As already noted, the Beast's covenant with Israel will be for seven years, but will be broken at the mid-point, implying two periods of three and a half years.
- Dan 12.7:- The fulfilment of "these wonders", when there shall be a time of trouble unprecedented in the world's history and when the power of Israel will be utterly shattered will be "time, times and half a time" (see also vv.1 & 6).
- Rev 11.2:- The court outside the latter day temple will be trodden by the Gentiles for forty-two months. We will consider problems associated with this temple in our next chapter.
- Rev 11.3:- God's two miraculously empowered witnesses will prophesy in Jerusalem clad in sackcloth for one thousand two hundred and sixty days.
- Rev 12.14:- The woman, representing Israel, will be given refuge in the wilderness from the Serpent for "a time and times and half a time".
- Rev 13.5:- The Beast is given authority to blaspheme and continue in office for forty-two months.

The expression 'a time, times and half a time' seems quaint to us, but was comprehended as a year, two years and half a year. Everything harmonises. It will become apparent later which three and a half year period of the above list is the first half of the seven, and which the second. The variety of expression used confirms that these cannot represent the Historicist's 1,260 years. They are indisputably the final detached seven years of Gabriel's prophecy for Daniel's people, Israel. They are not for the Church. After the Rapture we are going to have a heavenly view of these momentous events and are going to be intensely interested in how God is bringing to an end six thousand years of rebellion. The heavenly monitoring in Revelation of earthly happenings is instructive for us at any time. There are similar insights into this heavenly awareness in Daniel.

So we now have a well established seven year duration for these end-time events, a framework into which all the other events must fit. But again we must exercise some caution. We know the start point and the mid-point, but it is dangerous to assume that Jesus returns on precisely the final day of the seventh year. Satan does not dictate the day of the Lord's Coming in Power. Could He arrive marginally earlier? That is one possible interpretation of 'shortened' when Jesus said: "Unless those days were shortened, no flesh would be spared" (Matt 24.22); the Greek word means cut off, shortened or amputated. We will know one day, because we will be returning from Heaven with our Lord.

What has got to fit into this framework? We have a great many Day of Vengeance prophecies in the Old Testament, but these are often so interspersed with First Coming and Year of the Lord's Redeemed or Millennial prophecies that we need another starting point into which to fit the main building blocks. The great Northern invasion described in Ezekiel 38 and 39 and the closing chapters of Zechariah are notable exceptions. Most of Jesus' Olivet Discourse refers to this period.

As we try to fit revealed information together, let us recall something we mentioned in our first chapter. Earth is subject to time, which we more or less understand, having known nothing else. But time as we know it does not apply in Heaven, and it is doubtful whether any believer can at present fully grasp all the implications of the contrasting states. CS Lewis's Narnia books perhaps get as close to understanding as we are likely to achieve; it is a great pity that these brilliant children's books are so tarnished with ancient Greek mythology. The correlation between what happens in Heaven and earth may not be quite so simple as we assume and events on earth may not synchronise in quite the way or at quite the pace that we expect. However nothing on earth can pre-empt the heavenly authorisation.

BACK TO REVELATION

It is the book of Revelation which allows all other end-time prophecies to be fitted into a coherent framework: this does not mean that we can time every happening precisely. Some commentators can be very rash; but there is much which we can safely fit into a general progression. Every so often the sequence is interrupted to concentrate on personalities or scenes in Heaven or earth. However from Chapter 4 onwards there is an inexorable progress towards the triumphal return of the King of Kings and Lord of Lords. This will dramatically and decisively terminate the Day of Vengeance; He will deal with His enemies and usher in the Year of the Lord's Redeemed. Let us glance quickly now at the beginning and ending of Revelation to help us see the central part in context:-

- Rev 1: Introduction.
- Rev 2 & 3: Letters to seven contemporary congregations or assemblies.
- Rev 20: Satan's incarceration, the resurrection of the remainder of the saved, the thousand year Day of the Lord's Redeemed or Millennium, Satan's post-Millennial final challenge and consignment to Hell, the second resurrection (of the unsaved), the Great White Throne judgment of the unsaved.
- Rev 21 & 22: The new heaven and new earth.

This leaves the entire central part of the book, from the beginning of chapter 4 to the end of chapter 19, to cover the Day of Vengeance of our God. In the opening verses of Revelation, in the description of the glorified Lord, we find Christ's Coming in Power anticipated; "Behold, He is coming with clouds, and every eye will see Him, even they also who pierced Him. And all the tribes of the earth will also mourn because of Him" (1.7). Note the contrast of this coming with the joyful, comforting earlier description of the Rapture. How both the living and the dead will see Him, we are not told, but it is a statement of fact. Somehow even the souls as yet in Hades will be made aware of this stupendous event, just as, according to Isa 14.16, they will be able to gaze on Satan at his descent. But, though

Jesus' return is anticipated here, it is not accomplished until chapter 19, where we have the fullest account.

Jesus' personal instruction to John (Rev 1.19) is: "Write the things which you have seen, and the things which are, and the things which will take place after this." Jesus then delivers very personal letters to seven existing churches in the Roman province of Asia, in what we now call Turkey. The letters are salutary to Christians of all succeeding centuries. Jesus, who walks in the midst of the churches, identifies congregations who are full of works but loveless, who tolerate false teaching, who have a low opinion of themselves but are highly thought of by Him, who have a high opinion of themselves but have shut out their Lord, and so on. Every congregation of every age is duty bound to examine itself frequently. Reformation should not be a one in two thousand year event; it should be as often as it is needed.

Thereafter we find a voice commanding John to: "Come up here, and I will show you things which must take place after this" (4.1). This seems to pinpoint the Rapture within the Revelation sequence, although it does not actually say so in as many words. From then on we are in what is still future. Risen and glorified saints are seen crowned in Heaven. We are back at the point where the scene is set for the Seals to be opened and the Day of Vengeance to begin. Thereafter the vision alternates between the controlling scene in heaven and the consequent scene on earth. It is in Heaven that the seven Seals are broken which spark events on earth. Seven angels sound the trumpets which herald judgments on the inhabitants of the earth. Angels in Heaven pour out upon the earth the final Vials or Bowls of God's wrath. The three series of seven dominate the Day of Vengeance from beginning to end. But to place the three series end to end and then to fit all the other events into the resulting twenty gaps gives us complex and unnecessary problems. Let us look at them together, leaving the details until later.

HEAVENLY CONTROLS WITHIN THE DAY OF VENGEANCE
- Seven Seals (Rev 6.1 to 8.1), the first four of which send forth the Horsemen of the Apocalypse.
- Seven Trumpets (Rev 8.2 to 11.15), the last three of which are described as Woes.
- Seven Bowls of the wrath of God (Rev 16.1-21), most of which triple the intensity of the Trumpets.

We find that each of the three series takes us to a different aspect of the very end. It is important to be aware of this The opening of the sixth seal takes us to the catastrophic scene of powerful and mighty personages seeking to flee the presence of the Lamb by hiding in caves, while the seventh Trumpet takes us to the start of Christ's Millennial Kingdom. The seventh Bowl takes us to global earthquakes and upheavals and the destruction of man-made structures. The sequence is more comprehensible from Heaven than from earth. What does seem clear is that the three are coterminous, starting at different points but ending at more or less the same point. They serve as a guide. As we shall see in ensuing chapters, the Seals start at the beginning of the seven years, the Trumpets later in the first three and a half years and the Bowls towards the end of the latter three and a half. To pin-point them any more precisely and reach total consensus at present may be neither feasible not profitable. The start point of the Trumpets is perhaps the most difficult to determine,

For those who are preaching the Gospel at that time and for their converts, it will be of the greatest re-assurance and practical use in those dreadful days to know where they stand in God's timetable. God is gracious to His Tribulation saints in different ways compared with His present dealings with His Church. It is almost certain that the spectacular phenomena heralded by these signs will be used by God's witnesses at that time to validate and corroborate their message. They will be highly motivated students of prophecy!

God has not informed us of these grave matters for our entertainment. They have current applications to our attitudes to environmental concerns. Many churches show an almost criminal neglect of God's clearest warnings of impending ecological and cosmic disasters, not so much because we cannot avoid the inevitable, but because we can and should use them as a witness to the infallibility of Holy Scripture. Our young people are given earthly priorities and are left to share the worries of a godless world instead of having the confidence that Heaven rules and that things are on course. These are not days for Christians to remain silent.

What are more precisely fixed are the momentous events and the changes which are to take place at the crucial mid-point. As students of prophecy, we, or at least most of us, are prone to accept more readily the bliss of the Year of the Lord's Redeemed than we are the horrors of His Day of Vengeance. Scoffers "willingly forget" God's previous great world-wide judgment, "by which the world that then existed perished, being flooded with water. But the heavens and the earth which exist are kept by the same word (of God), are reserved for fire until the day of judgment and perdition of ungodly men" (II Pet 3.6-7).

There are parallels between the moral and rebellious conditions of mankind at the Flood and those of the Day of Vengeance, but there are also certain contrasts in God's dealings. Last time the Ark bore only eight aloft above the waters, whilst this time millions will be snatched away before disaster strikes. Last time death was instantaneous and global; this time, as we shall see, the Gospel witness will be word-wide, with accompanying signs, before the inevitable destruction of the unrepentant. "God is not willing that any should perish but that all should come to repentance" (II Pet 3.9). As we shall see, many will repent, but even more will not. Last time God made His rainbow-sealed covenant not to flood the earth again or to change the annual seasonal cycle before re-establishing humankind upon the earth (Gen 8.22, 9.11). Next time, having intervened at the point of earth's destruction (Matt 24.22), He will renew the shattered earth, but will personally rule it in righteousness with a rod of iron, until just before it is time to fold up for ever this doomed creation.

Just as we find it difficult to comprehend all the contrasts between the Acceptable Year, the Day of Vengeance and the Year of the Lord's Redeemed – or, if we prefer between what people assume to be the *status quo* and the worst and best case scenarios – so we may find it difficult to comprehend the difference between the first and second three-and-a-half year periods. Only when we see what is to happen at the half-way point can we begin to understand. However we dare not gamble with our salvation in the confidence that the first half of the Day of Vengeance will be less traumatic than the second. The first half will be bad enough, and, as we have already seen, once the cut-off point of the Rapture occurs, there can be no further offer of salvation, only an awful deception, for those who now consciously postpone getting right with God.

In our next chapter we will look at the first three and a half years in more detail.

CHAPTER FOUR

The Beginning of Sorrows

THE WISE SHALL UNDERSTAND

New Testament saints have a much clearer picture of the latter days than did Old Testament saints. We are able to look back to many prophecies which were fulfilled at the time of Jesus' First Coming, and forward to others which relate to the time of His Second Coming. They saw them all as future and were unable to discern between them. Progressively, through the age of modern technology, nuclear weapons and serious environmental concerns, certain prophecies have become more comprehensible than they were to our predecessors, though we must beware of explaining what is clearly miraculous in scientific terms. The spectacular history of Israel since the 1917 Balfour Declaration, with its providential preservation against overwhelming odds, has thrown further light on end time events. Thus understanding of prophecy does gradually increase. This unique survival is evidence provided by God of His purposes for Israel, evidence which makes the enemies of the Jews doubly guilty.

We have already noted some of the Bible's injunctions to heed prophecy, and have been encouraged by the blessings that are attached to such study, if done reverently and diligently. However before we try to fit prophecies into the two halves of the Day of Vengeance, let us take a precautionary look at the context of the prediction in Dan 12.10: "The wise shall understand". Full understanding of many end-time prophecies will not be available to saints on earth until those final seven years of tribulation. Even then they may be recognised only as they are happening. This will be part of God's encouragement to His saints at that dreadful time. It will also help to validate the message of the tribulation evangelists, whom we will discuss soon. In the meantime the wise of today may understand a great deal, but not everything. We are always permitted to know as much as we need, and sometimes a little extra.

We take at face value, as we must, Jesus' predictions of wars. We have noted that the rider of the red horse represents wars; but we do not have details of every conflict. From Nebuchadnezzar's dream we know about the Beast's kingdom as some sort of Revived Roman Empire, but we are as yet unsure of its boundaries or its constituent nations. Some predicted conflicts cannot be pinned down to a given point within the Day of Vengeance; others can be. Only one campaign is described in detail and one other in outline. We will look at these in due course. There are doubtlessly going to be wars in other parts of the globe which do not impinge directly on Israel, and are therefore not covered at all. What the Kings of the East do among themselves is a closed book to us - until they prepare to cross the Euphrates.

Once he has established his authority and assumed headship of the Revived Roman Empire, the Beast may control around a quarter or even a third of the world. It has been suggested that this is why so many Trumpet judgments apply to only a third of the world in contrast with the later global Bowls of Wrath; this may well be true. His empire is to be made up of ten kingdoms (Dan 7.24, Rev 17.12), but we cannot identify the kings individually. We know that their reign, subordinate to the Beast, will be very short, and that initially they will be under the influence of the great inter-faith religious harlot described as Mystery Babylon. Later we shall see how and why they will turn and destroy her. We think it rather unlikely that the Beast will gain world-wide obedience before the mid-point; towards the end of the Great Tribulation he is likely to lose some control.

Nothing seems to be said in the Bible about the Americas. The United States has been the most powerful nation on earth during the Twentieth Century. But this could all change. Evangelical Christians in the USA have wielded enormous influence over policies, particularly regarding Israel. But the vast majority of these will be raptured. A few natural disasters, such as a massive San Andreas Fault earthquake or more super-hurricanes or volcanic eruptions, could possibly revive the old Pan-American attitudes and lead to a partial withdrawal from world affairs. This is speculative. Certainly the Beast's empire, rather than any other bloc or power, is set to dominate the world scene eventually.

The European Community has undergone many changes recently. Many newer member states were never part of the old Roman Empire, and the former Soviet Union, having been dismembered, has lost to the Community several former satellites – not a happy state of affairs for Moscow. Could there be a massive re-shuffle after the Rapture? Again we do not know. However Russia does seem to feature in one end-time prophecy as a power quite distinct from the Revived Roman Empire. Could she regain some of her former republics and satellites? Could she enter into an alliance with Muslim neighbours against Israel? Ezekiel seems to throw some light on this question; we will consider this in some detail before the end of this chapter. In the meantime, let us concentrate on the many facts that are clear or at least clearer.

THE OLIVET DISCOURSE

The title of this chapter is taken from Jesus' Olivet Discourse. Only Jesus uses the term, 'The beginning of sorrows' (Matt 24.8). The Sermon on the Mount is recorded in one Gospel only; yet in many churches it is quoted and expounded very much more frequently than the Olivet Discourse, which is covered in three. In view of the fact that Jesus took time four days before His crucifixion, to deliver so long an address, and in view of the fact that the Holy Spirit inspired three Gospel writers to record it, one cannot but wonder in whose interests it is that, in these dark days, it should be thus sidelined. The Discourse is to be found in greater or lesser detail in Matthew 24 and 25, Mark 13 and Luke 21.

Unger's Bible Dictionary says, "In this prophetic statement of our Lord concerning Israel, there is no mention made of the church, her beginning, her course, her destiny or her sojourn in the world. Likewise no reference is made to the Person or work of the Holy Spirit as they occur in this age". It evidently refers to the time when the Church will no longer be on earth. Jesus gave His parting message, including a brief promise of His return, to the Church three days later, after He and His disciples had kept the Passover; and of course He had more to say to them after His resurrection. But after the Olivet Discourse He had no more to say whilst on earth about the nation which did not want Him to reign over it.

The timing of the Discourse is of the greatest significance. It followed Jesus' last visit – a formal and condemnatory visit – to the Temple, that sacred building which Herod the Great had enlarged and beautified, but which had originally been built by the returned exiles from Babylon, to replace Solomon's Temple, which had in turn replaced the Tabernacle which dated back to the exodus from Egypt. And the Tabernacle was built "according to the pattern shown you (Moses) on the mountain" (Heb 8.5). For all Israel's idolatry over the centuries, God was still intensely interested in His Temple at Jerusalem.

Matthew and Mark both tell how the disciples left the Temple, remarking on its beauty, and made their way to the Mount of Olives, where they privately questioned Jesus. All three record His statement, which had led to their enquiries, that not one stone would be left upon another. Only Mark tells us that it was Peter, Andrew, James and John who were present thereafter.

Between the three accounts all parts of the tripartite question of the disciples are answered. In verse 3 of Matthew's account we read: "Tell us, when will these things be? And what will be the sign of Your coming and of the end of the age?" "These things" refers back to Jesus' statement regarding the destruction of the temple. But the disciples assumed that this would occur at the same time as Jesus' return in glory. At this stage they did not perceive the intervening Church Age.

Only Luke gives any details of what Jesus said about the forthcoming destruction of Jerusalem (vv.20-25), in a passage which concludes with, "And they will fall by the edge of the sword, and be led away captive into all nations". That ends Luke's 70 AD section; the rest is future, although doubtlessly there has been much comfort obtained over the intervening years, because strife and troubles had been foretold by Jesus, rather than the moral and social progress which some believers still insist is the correct pattern.

That part which is covered in Matthew's Gospel is entirely to do with the future, and it is here we find three stages most clearly described, as noted by Dr Graham Scroggie:-
- Matt 24.4-14 – The first half of the seven years or Heptad of Dan 9.27 (Mk 13.4-13 and Lk 21.8-19 also refer).
- Matt 24.15-28 – The mid-point and second half of the Heptad (Mk 13.14-23 and Lk 21.20-24 also refer).
- Matt 24.29-31 and chap 25 – The end of the Heptad and preparation for the Year of the Lord's Redeemed (Mk 13.24-27 and Lk 21.25-28 also refer).

Preterists contend that most end time prophecies refer primarily, if not altogether, to events of the first two centuries. This leaves them with huge problems. While the sack of Jerusalem and dispersal of the Jews did indeed take place then, most of the other predictions simply did not occur at that time - unless Jesus was wildly exaggerating in the Discourse. To overcome this, they say that Jesus was indeed exaggerating, but justifiably, in order to emphasise the importance of the predictions!!! But to believe this is to open the flood-tides to endless abuse of interpretation. If this Discourse was exaggerated, why not the rest of Jesus' teaching? Are Jesus' birth, crucifixion and resurrection similarly exaggerated simply because they were important? God forbid! The authority of the Bible would be totally undermined. The Olivet Discourse exposes the bankruptcy of one of the leading diversions of our time, a diversion which allows faith in the miraculous in the distant past, but not the miraculous in the foreseeable future. That is hardly faith at all.

So we turn our attention to those verses in Matt 24.4-14, to discover more about the first half of the Heptad or first three and a half years. Key words are, "The end is not yet" (v.6) and "The beginning of sorrows" (v.8). Here we see a distinct period ending with the Abomination of Desolation. Compare this passage with Revelation chapter 6, and we are reminded of the sending out of the four horsemen. We start off with a warning of false Christs, by whom many will be deceived. Perhaps there is a reference here to individuals outside what is the Beast's first sphere of influence claiming to be messiahs within their own religious realms, taking advantage of the spiritual vacuum and bewilderment after the Rapture. In Dan 9.27 it is with 'the many' that the false covenant will be concluded – clearly the many who will be deceived. The proliferation of false prophets is also foretold, with claims somewhat less blasphemous than those of the false Christs (v.11).

THE REMAINING HORSEMEN

The second or red horseman is reflected in verses 6 and 7: "Wars and rumours of wars...for nation shall rise against nation and kingdom against kingdom". The Greek for nation here is *ethne*, and could equally mean that ethnic groups will rise against one another – sadly the trend is already here. However much these features have been true in the past, there will be an intensification of them within the first three and a half years in the build up to the later Great Tribulation. We suspect that these conflicts will include what in military terms one might call 'messy wars', with terrorism and genocide rather than clear demarcation of sides. Such traditional conventions as rules of engagement and acceptable conduct are already almost a thing of the past. But under the first Seal one personality, the Beast, is given temporary authority, with a victor's crown or wreath, *stephanos*, sent out "conquering and to conquer" (Rev 6.2); his short term victory is permitted by Heaven. His arrowless bow may indicated conquest with limited bloodshed. However it is the rider with the great sword on the following red horse (Rev 6.4) who has "power to take peace from the earth". We seem to have a progression from geo-political posturing, manipulation and coercion to all-out open warfare.

The black horseman of the third Seal brings famine. To appreciate the Revelation description, it is helpful to know that "a quart of wheat for a denarius" means a day's pay for wheaten bread, or that the same money will buy three times as much of a cheaper grain. But the overall picture is of serious food shortages, particularly with staple items. Jesus in His Discourse (Matt 24.7) simply says that there will be famine. Already we are familiar with the frightening statistics of the undernourished and starving of our planet. This will be worse and more widespread after the Rapture. When we consider the consequences of the ensuing Trumpets and Bowls with their catastrophic environmental effects, we see that famine on an unprecedented scale can be the only consequence. Reduced sunshine, parched earth, lifeless oceans, totally devastated cereal crops, grass and fruit trees will all play their part. Hunger itself exacerbates conflict, as starving armies seek to conquer and plunder lands which they suppose to be less impoverished than their own. From 6:6 we see that luxury items will be less affected than staple foodstuffs; this again will be cause for jealousy and contention. Not only will the effects of the four Seals be individually discernible, but collectively they will interact with each other to multiply suffering.

The fourth horse is a sickly pale green. The name of its rider is "Death, with Hades following" (Rev 6.8), with power to kill by a variety of means a quarter of the world's population. This does not necessarily mean that these will all die in the first three and a half years. As we have already remarked, once each horse and rider has gone forth, its task does not have to conclude immediately, but can carry on into the second period. There is much evidence in Revelation that the majority of the deaths are to occur later. Jesus sums up the threat to life simply by saying (Matt 24.22) that only God's direct intervention at the end will prevent total loss of life. This partly answers the often asked question of whether the Great Tribulation is the result of God's decrees or of man's own suicidal use of weapons of mass destruction and of violations of our God-given environment. Most commentators would probably agree that both are contributory: either way, unrepentant mankind will get what it deserves. Having considered the four horsemen, let us now deal with what some people see as a major problem with prophecies which touch on the Temple.

THE PERCEIVED PROBLEM OF THE REBUILT TEMPLE

Some Bible students are not at all happy about the idea of a future Temple in Jerusalem. How, they ask, in the light of what we learn in the book of Hebrews, can there be a future Temple recognised by God? They point out that there has been no Temple in Jerusalem since the Romans destroyed it in 70 AD. The Temple site is occupied by the Al Aqsa Mosque is it not? Over the last few decades, in a city never actually named in the pages of the Koran, this has suddenly and emotively been claimed as the third most sacred place in Islam. Any attempt to rebuild a Jewish Temple would raise an outcry which would rock the Muslim world. All these objections seem reasonable. But let us not forget that in Ezra's day opposition to the rebuilding of the Temple from surrounding nations was equally strong; yet God's will prevailed. If the Bible says there will be a latter-day Temple, a latter-day Temple there will be; if it does not there will not be one.

The chances of a Temple being built or at least started before the Rapture seem slim, but cannot be ruled out on prophetic grounds; the components and equipment have already been prepared and are available. One can visualise various possibilities, such as a cruise missile from a Muslim neighbour state going slightly astray and taking out the Dome on the Rock, or a defiant Israel being in a position of such military strength as to decide unilaterally to build the Temple on the original site to the north of the Dome. However, the fact that after the Rapture Israel is to enter into a covenant agreement with the Beast suggests that in the interim period, far from being in a security position to take such a risk, they will become more rather than less vulnerable. At the predicted time the covenant with the Beast or 'prince that is to come' will seem to be the only option.

The Beast's seven year covenant demands a Temple, for Jews would never resume the sacrifices and offerings except in the Temple (Dan 9.27); this is why they have never previously been re-commenced. Only the Passover is celebrated elsewhere, namely within homes. The Abomination of Desolation spoken of by Daniel is to stand in the Holy Place (Matt 24.15 – and the Gospel writer adds "whoever reads, let him understand"). Mark 13.14 adds Jesus' words that the Abomination will "stand where it ought not to"; that is significant. In Dan 8.13-14 such desecration of the Temple in a latter day setting is confirmed by Gabriel; the defiled sanctuary is predicted to be cleansed after the Great Tribulation. God would hardly order the cleansing of an irrelevant temple. In II Thess 2.4 we are told that the Beast will actually sit as God in the Temple of God, showing himself that he is God. In Rev 11.1 we are told that the outer court will be given to the Gentiles. This is interesting, because if this Temple is correctly sited, the existing Mosque would be within that area which is said to be given to the Gentiles. It is feasible that the two could exist side by side for a while. How the world would applaud! How people like to approve religious compromise in defiance of God's laws! The Beast who brokered the deal would gain global admiration.

Orthodox Jews have already prepared to rebuild the Temple almost at lightening speed at the first opportunity. But as it is to function as part of an arrangement made with the Beast, there will certainly be no Shekinah glory. Its ordinances and ceremonies will be hollow and meaningless. It will be managed by a religious hierarchy at least as unspiritual as the one of Jesus' time on earth. But it will still be God's Temple on God's site in the city which He has chosen.

The Temple of Jesus' time was known as Herod's Temple. The sanctuary and main building were the work of Ezra, but many of the eye-catching additions were done by the Edomite Herod the Great. Yet Jesus said that it was His Father's house, the place to which He was taken at His circumcision, and publicly recognised by Simeon and Anna. It was the place where, even at the age of twelve, He was involved in His Father's business (Lk 2.49). It was from the temple, His "Father's house", that He later angrily drove out the money changers (Jn 2.14-18), making the disciples recall the words of Ps 69.9: "Zeal for Your house has eaten me up". God has recognised one imperfect temple; He can and will recognise another.

Of course the Temple ritual, originally ordained by God, has been obsolete since Calvary (Heb 8.13). Of course the veil rent from top to bottom signified that the way into the true Holy of Holies had been opened up through Jesus offering His own blood and entering Heaven as our High Priest (Heb 9.11, 24, 28 & 10.14-22). Of course the time has come when "you will neither on this mountain, nor in Jerusalem, worship the Father" (Jn 4.21). Of course there is an undefiled true Temple in Heaven as well as at times an earthly one.

And yet God told Solomon, "I have chosen Jerusalem, that My name may be there" (II Chron 6.5), even though in the same passage (v.18), Solomon recognised that the Temple had its limitations: "Will God indeed dwell with men on earth? Behold, heaven and earth cannot contain You. How much less this temple which I have built?" We have a pair of contrasting truths, neither of which can be ignored. Thus we know that, "The hour is coming and now is, when the true worshipers will worship the Father in spirit and in truth" (Jn 4.23).

The apostles still regarded the desecrated Temple at Jerusalem as God's house even after the veil had been rent in two when Jesus died. Peter and John went there at the hour of prayer (Acts 3.1). Paul went there in connection with a vow at the end of his third missionary journey, even although, in a cutting but appropriate remark, he indicated that he did not recognise the legitimacy of the High Priest (Acts 21.26 and 23.1-5).

Malachi's prophecy was only partially fulfilled at Jesus' first coming: "The Lord whom you seek, will suddenly come to His Temple, even the Messenger of the covenant, in whom you delight. 'Behold, He is coming,' says the Lord of Hosts" (Mal 3.1). If we read on a little, we are left in no doubt that this refers primarily to His Second Coming and to Israel's refining judgment and ultimate restoration. In fact this prophecy of Malachi follows immediately that challenge to contemporary Israel: "You have wearied the Lord with your words; yet you say 'In what way have we wearied Him?' In that you say 'Everyone who does evil is good in the sight of the Lord, and He delights in them,' or 'Where is the God of justice'?" (2.17). There is an obstinacy today to recognise that Israel's worst Holocaust lies ahead. Moreover, some Christians, notably Post-Millennialists, are determined to believe that God's Day of Vengeance for the world can be by-passed. This is dangerous and wrong; we are too easily influenced by psychologists and political activists with New Age leanings.

Much publicity has been given to the fact that some evangelical Christians are not only giving moral support to Israel, which in general is praiseworthy, but are encouraging the rebuilding of the Temple and in some cases contributing financially. This is misguided, as it suggests that they recognise the on-going validity of the now obsolete Levitical sacrifices and ritual for which it is designed. It is aiding and abetting a dead cause and detracting from the truth of the New Covenant which all believers have if they are in Christ.

This rebuilt Temple must not be confused with the future great Millennial Temple referred to in Mic 4.2 and Zech 14.16-21 and described in Ezekiel's closing chapters. This is simply a premature, short lived Temple which many prophecies assure will exist in Jerusalem during the Day of Vengeance of our God, in both the Beginning of Sorrows and the Great Tribulation. Its builders will intend it to be the replacement for previous temples; overtly it will be seen to be such. However, because it is to be on God's temple site, He will judge those who desecrate it.

GOD'S WITNESSES IN THE DAY OF VENGEANCE

The fifth Seal does not reveal a horse and rider. Rather it shows beneath the heavenly altar the souls of the Tribulation martyrs. We have already seen that the sixth Seal refers to the end of the Great Tribulation, so it is not unreasonable to assume that these are the souls of believers who have been slain at any time within the seven years. Their resurrection will not take place until after the Lord's Return in Power (Rev 20.4), but their souls and spirits will have been arriving in Heaven from probably quite soon after the Rapture until the end of the Great Tribulation. They will of course be fully conscious (Rev 6.10).

In verses 9 to 12 of Matthew 24, Jesus switches from the destruction and suffering of the world to the position of His disciples at that time: "Then they will deliver you up to tribulation and kill you, and you will be hated by all nations for My name's sake…and because lawlessness will abound, the love of many will grow cold". There are always loud protests when one points out that the falling away has already started. This is 'negative', we are told. However it is also Scriptural; it is expressly taught by the Holy Spirit in I Tim 4.1-2 and confirmed in II Tim 4.3-4. We have Old Testament precedents. There were splendid revivals in the times of Hezekiah and Josiah, but the prophets vociferously confirmed the underlying evil trend, and these revivals were unable to prevent the

Babylonian captivity. Revival is still an option until the moment of the Rapture; we should not be deterred for praying for it.

Now a very reasonable question to ask at this point is who Jesus was referring to by 'you' in these verses, assuming that the entire Church is to be raptured before the Day of Vengeance starts. He was addressing a small group of apostles, those whom He had commissioned to preach; they also all happened to be Jews, and He warned them that they will be killed and hated at a time when many will be offended and love will grow cold. Jesus said that they will be hated by all nations for His name's sake; already Jews are hated by far more nations than any other race. Already ordinary Gentile Christians, particularly those taking a strong moral stand, are being increasingly marginalised and ostracised; the trend is very evident.

Jesus said: "This Gospel of the Kingdom will be preached in all the world as a witness to all the nations, and then the end will come" (v.14). Now there has been since the time of Abel only one means of salvation, which is through the blood of the Lord Jesus Christ. Every soul recorded in the Roll Call of Faith (see Hebrews 11) and every soul added since is saved the same way, "For there is no other name under Heaven given among men by which we must be saved" (Acts 4.12). However there was a change of emphasis and a much greater level of understanding after Pentecost. John the Baptist had emphasised repentance above all, with the Kingdom of God at hand (Matt 3.1-11). So apparently it will be during the Day of Vengeance. The term 'Gospel of the Kingdom' is not found in the epistles.

The Church will not be available. She will be in Heaven with her Lord, where, having been the espoused Bride of Christ, she will, following the Bema or appraisal judgment of believers, become the glorified and consummated Bride (Rev 19.7). We have already seen that the Church succeeded the nation Israel in the central place of God's favour, and that when the Church Age is over, Israel must return to that central place in God's plans for the earth. But the prophecies of the restoration of Israel which we have seen so far refer not to the Day of Vengeance but to the Year of the Lord's Redeemed. We seem to have a problem. Israel is to be blind and largely unrepentant until she sees her Messiah return. Yet, whether consciously or by default, she is still witnessing to God's faithfulness. "Yet hear now, O Jacob My servant, and Israel whom

I have chosen. Thus says the Lord who made you...Thus says the Lord, the King of Israel...'You are My witnesses'" (Isa 44.1-2, 6-8). Sadly it is recorded that, far from being a credit to God in this role, they regularly brought His name into disrepute.

But we have here, during the Beginning of Sorrows. a faithful Jewish minority dispersed throughout the world and suffering martyrdom, quite distinct from a loveless and faithless majority. The original apostles had two roles. They were representative of the faithful minority within Israel, and were soon to be the nucleus of an overwhelmingly Gentile Church. Here Jesus is addressing them in their Jewish role. Of course the original apostles will be risen and in glory by this time. So they must have latter day successors who can preach the Gospel of the Kingdom to a world in its final throes of rebelliousness. Can Revelation help us? Yes it can.

We turn now to Revelation chapter 7, which Hal Lindsey describes as "a parenthetical panorama of the evangelistic activity of the Tribulation period" (There's a New World Coming). Following the opening of the first six Seals, but before their destructive effects are felt, we find an angel possessing God's seal crying to the four angels delegated with destruction of the earth and sea: "Do not harm the earth, the sea, or the trees till we have sealed the servants of our God on their foreheads" (Rev 7.2-3). So here, after the Church has been taken to Heaven, and evidently very early in the first three and a half years, we find God's specially authorised angel setting apart people who have not previously been sealed. Within the Church, of course, all believers are sealed by the Holy Spirit from the moment of their salvation (Eph 1.13).

They are described in Rev 7.4-8. There are a hundred and forty-four thousand of them and they are drawn from the twelve tribes of Israel. Some people find this very difficult, but it is clearly stated in the form of an end-time prophecy; God's Holy Spirit wants us to be informed. We need not go into a detailed discussion about why certain tribes are included or excluded. We know that there was never a mass return of the ten tribes from Assyria and that indeed some tribes seem to have disappeared; but can we not trust the God who designed DNA to know who, wherever they are in the world, belongs to each tribe?

Early Russelites, fancifully calling themselves 'Jehovah's Witnesses', claimed to be the 144,000; when their numbers topped this figure they had to do a quick revision of their teachings! The fact that this cult was wrong is no reason for us to shun an important revelation. The number has been taken by some to be symbolic. We talked earlier about symbolic numbers, but found that where precise numbers are given they seem to be exactly what is stated. It is possible to be both precise and symbolic, as with the twelve Apostles. What is important is that God is to seal a very large number of Jews, though they will still be less than one percent of world Jewry. Early in the seven years, immediately following this and before the seventh Seal is opened, John was shown, in stark contrast to the 144,000, an immense multitude of the redeemed from every tribe, people and language standing before the Lamb and praising God. There is no doubt about *their* identity. John was told: "These are the ones who come out of the Great Tribulation, and washed their robes and made them white in the blood of the Lamb" (Rev 7.14). Now John is evidently seeing all the Tribulation saints here, except the 144,000. What we have in Revelation 7 are firstly the evangelists and secondly their converts.

The emphatic Jewish identification of the 144,000 at this future point is eloquent confirmation that the mainly Gentile Church is to be in glory with her Lord. This confirms a Pre-Tribulation Rapture. Had the Rapture been Post-Tribulation, the existing Church could have continued to win souls; no nationality would have had to be given. God has gone out of His way here to emphasise what to the Replacement Theologian is a distasteful truth; God still has crucial roles for Jews.

Why will they not have been raptured with the Church, as any other saved Jew would be? The answer must be that they will be neither saved nor sealed until after the Rapture. They will be devout and zealous men, known intimately to God. We strongly suspect that they will be a sincere minority of rabbis and others who honour God with their hearts but who will yet have to recognise their true Messiah. We may assume that the Rapture will have a huge impact upon them. Perhaps at that point they will be compelled to search their consciences and give opportunity for the Holy Spirit to lighten them, as Saul of Tarsus was once enlightened from a position of blind zeal (Phil 3.6). Ezekiel, at the time when the Lord's Shekinah glory was about to depart from the Temple, sent an angel to "put a mark on the foreheads of the men who sigh and cry over all the abominations that are done within" (Ezek 9.4). We are not told whether the mark will be visible to others.

No doubt they will be steeped in the Old Testament Scriptures. No doubt previously they will have had "a zeal for God, but not according to knowledge" (Rom 10.2). The Holy Spirit will be able to supplement immediately such knowledge, as He did with Paul and other early converts, to enable them to "preach Christ, and Him crucified". They will be distinct from their unspiritual colleagues who will be deceived into entering into the covenant of Dan 9.27 with the Beast.

These witnesses are to be commissioned, as were the twelve in Matt 10.1, except inasmuch as their ministry will no longer be confined to "the lost sheep of the house of Israel" (Matt 10.6). Rather, "Their sound has gone out to all the earth, and their words to the ends of the world" (Rom 10.18). The reception of their message will differentiate between the 'sheep' and the 'goats' in a passage which we have yet to look at (Matt 25.32 et seq). Peter on the day of Pentecost recalled Joel's prophecy (Joel 2.28-32 with Acts 2.16 & 21). On that memorable occasion much was fulfilled, but not the words, "And I will show wonders in the heavens and in the earth; blood and fire and pillars of smoke, the sun shall be turned into darkness, and the moon into blood, before the coming of the great and awesome day of the Lord, and it shall come to pass that whoever calls on the name of the Lord shall be saved". Next time the postponed portion also will be fulfilled; we assume that the Gospel will be preached in every local tongue through the power of the Holy Spirit, as it was to the Jewish pilgrims gathered at Jerusalem at Pentecost.

Joel continues beyond Peter's citation of him, taking his readers up to Armageddon and to the Lord's Return in Power. So the witness of these evangelists seems to continue throughout the seven years. Opinions are divided as to whether none, some or all will be martyred, but all will endure great privation; "I was a stranger and you did not take Me in, naked and you did not clothe Me, sick and in prison and you did not visit Me...inasmuch as you did not do it to one of the least of these, you did not do it to Me" (Matt 25.43-45). Those addressed by Jesus here are clearly stated to be those alive and on earth at His return (Matt 25.31), not the dead. *Their* judgment comes much later. He is going to be judging those who, during the previous few years, have heard the Gospel preached by them, and who have responded either positively or negatively. In the opening verses of Revelation 14 we see these evangelists at the end of the Great Tribulation standing victoriously with the Lamb. They have been called 144,000 Paul's, Billy Graham's and other suitable titles; but surely the loveliest is simply "these My brethren" (Matt 25.40) – Jesus' own special personal recognition.

Their converts are the martyrs, who cry: "How long, O Lord, holy and true, until You judge and avenge our blood on those who dwell on the earth?" (Rev 6.10). This is a very different attitude to our Saviour's "Father, Forgive them, for they know not what they do" (Lk 23.34) or Stephen's plea, "Lord, do not charge them with this sin" (Acts 7.60). But this is the Day of Vengeance; the Acceptable Year of the Lord's forbearance is over. God's vengeance will surely follow. The call for vengeance will no longer be inappropriate. Appeals for justice, assumed by many never to have been unanswered, as so many Psalms reflect, will now be dealt with speedily.

FURTHER WITNESSES

In Revelation 11 we read: "And I will give power to My two witnesses, and they will prophesy one thousand two hundred and sixty days, clothed in sackcloth" (v.3). We then read of their supernatural power to destroy their opponents and of their ability to bring down judgments on the earth. There is no indication that these are symbolic figures. They are actual latter day prophets – extraordinary men for extraordinary times. No doubt the 144,000 will be glad to be able to quote them, so well known (and unpopular) will they be. Their stance will be the Temple precincts in Jerusalem. Their accreditation will be divine. Their testimony will coincide with the first three and a half years. As soon as the Beast's covenant is accepted by the duped religious and civil authorities in Jerusalem, it will be publicly denounced by them; they will warn the city of what is happening and about to happen.

Good arguments have been presented for these being Enoch and Elijah, two men who have never previously died. But when we consider that millions will be raptured without tasting death, this somewhat weakens the case without destroying it. Others think that it will be Moses and Elijah; only God knows where Moses is buried, and Satan must have had good reason to be anxious to have access to his body (Jude 1.9). Elijah has been promised to return to Israel "Before the coming of the great and dreadful day of the Lord" (Mal 4.5); John the Baptist, the earlier potential Elijah, in his day was welcomed by many individuals, but rejected by the nation. Whoever they will turn out to be, they too will have many converts, but at the end of their tour of duty they will be slain by the Beast (v.7) to the delight of their enemies world-wide, whose consciences will have been blasted for forty-two months. Three and a half days later they are going to be resurrected and visibly caught up into heaven (vv.11-12). Nobody else is said to be raptured at this juncture.

THE GOG AND MAGOG INVASION OF EZEKIEL

What is generally known as the Gog and Magog invasion of Israel, as foretold in Ezekiel chapters 38 and 39, is one of those areas where we have to be particularly careful, because the actual timing within the latter days is not stated. We will leave the identity of Gog until later in this chapter; suffice it to say at this stage that the majority of commentators have thought that this is Russia, but a growing minority believes that it is an Islamic country or ruler, perhaps from the former USSR.

Looking firstly at Chapter 38, we learn that that the invasion is indisputably a latter day one – "after many days...in the latter years" (v.8). This is confirmed by the historical fact that no such invasion as that so carefully described here has ever occurred, yet it is stated quite emphatically by God (vv.1-2) that it will happen. Once again we are reminded that God still has a vast amount of unfinished business with Israel.

- The scale of the invasion will be vast – "like a cloud to cover the land" (v.8, also vv.6 & 16).
- The aims of this invasion will include land acquisition and plunder (v.11).
- International opposition or challenge to the invasion will be merely verbal (v.13). Whether this is because of complicity, inability, apathy or preoccupation with other matters, we are not told. Allowing your enemies to sap their strength elsewhere is an age-old strategy.
- Sovereign God will sanction this invasion; He specifically sets His face against Gog (vv.1 & 16). He reveals to us though Ezekiel His personal agenda in this matter. He is now about to accomplish things which His wise forbearance has hitherto delayed.
- The routing of the invasion force will be dramatic, decisive and

manifestly miraculous, leading to world-wide recognition of God's personal involvement (vv.3 & 16). "Thus I will magnify Myself and sanctify Myself; and I will be known in the eyes of many nations. Then they shall know that I am the Lord" (v.23).

- These divine manifestations – true Acts of God - will include a gigantic earthquake in an area (v.19), which has been arranged by Him, probably at the time of the Flood, to lie astride one of the world's greatest fault systems.
- The earthquakes will be accompanied by such phenomena as flooding, hailstones and plague (v.22). Again we see links with Revelation.
- Just as when Gideon's select three hundred faced the Midianite host (Judg 7.22), the invaders will destroy each other (v.21), without Israel lifting a finger. Israel will thus not be given the credit; God will reserve that for Himself.
- Moving onto chapter 39, we note that, whilst the invading forces will not fall until they reach the mountains of Israel, their homelands will not escape God's wrath (v.6).
- Israel will plunder the equipment abandoned by the invaders (vv.9-10). The fact that these weapons are described in ancient terms should not be a problem to the serious reader, who will recognise that the passage has had to make sense to readers for over two and a half thousand years, most of whom knew nothing of pyrotechnics, let alone modern technology.
- The fallen will be given a burial site within Israel; the place will thereafter be suitably named as a reminder and memorial (v.11).

THE TIMING OF THE INVASION

Even theologians who are well nigh unanimous about the timing of other latter day events are divided over this particular issue. We include the invasion in this chapter because we believe that this is the timing which best suits the details given. However it is only one of three main options:-

- Before the Rapture.
- During the first half of the seven years or Beginning of Sorrows.
- At the end of the Great Tribulation, as a prelude to or part of the Armageddon campaign.

It may just be that this invasion will happen before the Rapture, but we believe this to be very unlikely indeed, because it is to take place when Israel is unarmed and feels secure, and we do not expect that to happen before the Beast's false seven year treaty (Dan 9.27). Hitherto such a peace settlement has evaded the world's brightest politicians. Also it gives rise to one enormous problem. It turns the Gog and Magog invasion into a prerequisite for the Rapture. We are convinced that there are no known prerequisites.

A more serious contender is at or near the end of the Great Tribulation, either as a prelude to or actually as part of the Battle of Armageddon. There are indeed to be mighty earthquakes at the time of Armageddon. However Ezekiel gives no hint whatsoever of the visible arrival upon the scene of the conquering Messiah, which is the central event at that juncture. In this campaign God is to be recognised, not because "every eye shall see Him", but because of the manner of the defeat. The repentance of the survivors of Israel is graphically described in Zechariah 12 at the time of the Lord's return, but the defeat of God and Magog is not shown there as a reason. This also points to its being a separate earlier event.

We know from Matt 24.21 that the Great Tribulation will be unprecedented in earth's history, and from Daniel 12.1 that Israel will be at the centre of this. This will be the time of the utter global devastation ensuing from the cumulative effect of Seals, Trumpets and Bowls of Wrath. Yet Ezekiel tells us that the invasion will be at a time of peace for Israel. There are only two times of peace and prosperity ahead for Israel, (a) following the false messiah's covenant early in the seven years and (b) under the true Messiah's righteous reign in the Year of the Lord's Redeemed. The build up to Armageddon is emphatically not such a time.

The main argument for the later timing is based upon the closing verses of the passage (39.21-29), where God will be glorified among the nations and forever recognised by Israel (39.21-22). However there seems to be a natural break between the end of the prediction of the invasion (v.20) and these verses. The spectacular destruction of the invading forces by Divine intervention will be a timely challenge for the rest of the world, forcing people either to repent and risk martyrdom, or to remain unrepentant and soon accept the Mark of the Beast, which will put all recipients beyond hope of redemption (Rev 14.9-10). For some recognition will occur only at the very end of the Great Tribulation, when it will be far too late for those bearing the number of the Beast to repent. Only then will the whole world recognise for better or worse God's hand in everything. "The fool has said in his heart, 'There is no God'" (Ps 14.1). The fool so hardens his heart and brainwashes himself into being unable to see God's hand, no matter how powerfully it is displayed. The time will come when God will forcibly enlighten all such fools.

Sometime within the first half of the seven years is the timing which seems best to fit the details given. We suggest that the Beast's covenant or treaty will be rigidly enforced initially, because complete disarmament of that currently superbly disciplined, trained and equipped defence force of Israel is implied by Ezek 38.11 – "a land of unwalled villages..... a peaceful people, who dwell safely". Obviously some time will have to elapse for disarmament to take place. Now here is a highly probable scenario for the invasion – the prosperity of a nation free from the heavy economic burden of defence, feeling totally secure for the first time since Solomon's reign. In such circumstances Satan's other client, Gog, can at last take advantage of Israel's unprecedented defencelessness, relying on the Beast's empire's token protest (Ezek 38.13). Satan could cynically manipulate this. This would fit in with the second Seal or red horse of war. Time would be left in this programme for the burial of bodies and for the utilisation of abandoned equipment described by Ezekiel.

The fickleness or cynicism of the Beast in not standing by his treaty obligations need not surprise us. Israel of old made a number of disastrous unholy defensive alliances with nations or kings who subsequently failed them. God heard their reasoning: "We have made a covenant with death, and with Sheol we are in agreement. When the overflowing scourge passes through it will not come to us, for we have made lies our refuge, and under falsehood we have hidden ourselves" (Isa 28.15). God declares (v.18): "Your covenant with death will be annulled, and your agreement with Sheol will not stand".

WHO IS GOG?

In the prophetic context, we are told by Jesus to look at the fig tree (Israel) and all the trees (other nations) (Lk 21.29). We should keep a close eye on the nations, particularly in relationship to Israel. Sometimes we have to revise our ideas; this is entirely appropriate. For many years the majority of commentators have believed that Gog is Russia. Even before the 1917 Russian Revolution respected commentators like William Kelly argued that the reference was to Russia (Notes on Ezekiel). We will therefore look at this option first.

From 1917 until about 1990, much was made by prophetic writers of the overt godlessness of the Soviet Union. With its persecution of Christians and Jews, it seemed right for the Gog role. It allied itself with various Middle Eastern regimes which were opposed to the West, and was one of Israel's bitterest critics. Jews were ostracised in Russia at least as far back as the 15th Century. A hundred years later Ivan the Terrible ordered that those who would not convert to Christianity should be drowned. Later Jews in some major cities were confined to certain western areas or pales, and then to city ghettoes. The Pogroms of the 19th century were second only to the later German Holocaust in infamy. Even the Russian Orthodox Church was involved. So there really is a good case for Gog to be associated with Russia, and for God to deal with that nation in judgment. Both devout Jews and Christians persecuted during the Communist regime must have been comforted by this prophecy.

But the Soviet system has collapsed, and the Russian Orthodox Church has regained much influence since then; whatever Russia is, it is no more atheist than many other nominally Christian countries.

In Russia for hundreds of years there has been a sense of isolationism. Joining forces, particularly in a leadership role with other nations with a different agenda could rid her of the preoccupation and sometime obsession with *okryzheniye* or encirclement. For around sixty years she enjoyed super-power status, and her present maverick administration has suffered something of an identity crisis through the reduction of her sphere of influence. Perhaps the situation will become clearer before the Rapture; we do not know. The time will come when those living in Israel will be in no doubt whatsoever.

Ezekiel tells us that Gog is to be from the uttermost or remotest north. Moscow, 1,600 miles away, is within a degree or two of being directly north of Jerusalem, so geographically Russia is still a strong contender. However Unger's Dictionary points out that sometimes in the Old Testament armies from the east or north-east which approached by the Fertile Crescent route, as most did, rather than crossing the desert, were said to be from the north; that was the Jewish perception. On this basis even Afghanistan would qualify!

Gog is clearly a person, probably a title rather than a name. Magog, Meshech and Tubal (38.2) seem to be directly subordinate to Gog, whereas Persia, Cush and Put (v.5) and Gomer and Togarmah (v.6) appear to be allies. Togarmah is from the utmost north (v.6), as are Meshech and Tubal (39.2). Some have made much of the word *Rosh* (38.2-3, 39.1) as indicating Russia. However the *Rus* from which Russia is derived is a later word, describing the Swedish Vikings who, in the 8th to 10th centuries AD, developed trading posts between the Baltic and Constantinople, founding Novgorod and Kiev. *Rosh* actually meant prince, as the AV and Jewish Bibles render it, and is less likely to be a place or tribal name. One simply cannot be certain.

Meshech and Tubal are popularly but questionably identified as Moscow (*Moskva*) and Tobol'sk. The latter, though once a centre for Siberian expansion, is now a long way down the league table of major Russian cities. Its name is not ancient. The Moschi and Tibareni tribes, which the ancient Greeks identified with the Caucasus, seem more likely to correspond.

Some of the names, Gomer, Magog, Meshech and Tubal are listed in Gen 10.2 as sons of Japheth; we know that, following the Babel defiance (Gen 11.8), the families of Japheth spread generally northwards and also into Europe. But there have since been mass migrations and uprooting of populations; so ancient identifications of peoples are of only limited value, though named places do not generally move. Certainly some of these names, notably Magog, were identified in ancient times with the Scythians, a group of tribes who lived in a wide area between the Danube delta and the Caspian.

Now up to this point we have considered this alliance in terms of names. But what about the ideologies, cultures and other factors which might inspire this sudden co-operation for an unprovoked latter day invasion of Israel?

If we consider the other states listed in Ezekiel 38 and ask ourselves what they have in common, we are likely to come up with the single answer

– Islam! Iran, Libya and most of north-east Africa are Islamic and sworn opponents of Israel for religious reasons. Togarmah, whether it is in Turkey or Central Asia, is likewise Islamic. Russia for centuries has been at loggerheads with Islamic states on its borders. Any Soviet alliances of the 20th Century with Islamic states have been for economic or political purposes, rather than because of any mutual affection. But within the present CIS or former USSR, lying to the far north or north- east of Israel and thus fitting Ezekiel's description, are four Islamic republics, namely Azerbaijan, Kazakhstan, Uzbekistan and Turkmenistan.

Of the four listed, Kazakhstan in particular still has huge stockpiles of Soviet arms. Could it be that this great latter day invasion is exclusively of Muslim states? Will God at this point deal as decisively with Islam as He will in turn deal with the mainly apostate Christian realm of the Revived Roman Empire, the Beast's kingdom? Will Mystery Babylon be apostate Christianity and Gog militant Islam, equally reserved by God for wrath?

Over the past decade or so the rise of militant and fundamentalist Islam, with its quite unbelievably vitriolic hatred of Israel and its almost equally venomous loathing of the so-called Christian nations has shaken the world's political balance and its institutions. Islamic fundamentalists expect a holy war or *jihad*. Could this be it? Could Gog even be the awaited 12th Imam or Mahdi? The Iranians insist that this jihad, which they say is to sweep through certain recalcitrant Muslim states and ultimately eliminate Israel, is imminent. But nothing can happen until Israel's God and ours sanctions it. Should Gog's invasion indeed transpire to be the expected holy war, it seems inconceivable that a non-Muslim country or leader should head it. These are exciting times and should keep us on our toes. Such questions must remain at least at the back of our minds in view of the very fluid Middle East situation. There is a huge temptation to digress, but these issues are really best dealt with in journals such as Believer's Magazine or Prophetic Witness which can keep nearly up-to-the-minute. Books sadly tend to be out of date before they are published.

Three of Gog's allies are clearly identifiable, as they refer to geographical locations rather than to inhabitants. Persia is Iran, Put is roughly Libya in North Africa and is sometimes translated thus; Cush, shown in some Bibles as Ethiopia, equates to upper Egypt and lower Sudan; Sudan is currently bitterly opposed to Israel. We do not know whether Ezekiel's list of allies is exhaustive or not; the named ones might possibly also be representative of countries in their hinterlands. At the time of writing, Iran's frenetic posturing and quest for a man-made 'apocalypse' is putting that nation in line to receive God's wrath.

When one puts all these identifiable allies of Gog on a blank map, one is struck by the spaces that exist immediately to the north and south of Israel. This is probably explained by the fact that the war described in Daniel 11 between the King of the North and King of the South just before Armageddon will involve nations with military hardware, troops and capability, who were not wiped out with Gog's allies, occupying those spaces. We will review this conflict in chapter 6. It all seems to fit together and to confirm the earlier date for the Gog and Magog campaign.

OTHER EVENTS IN THE BEGINNING OF SORROWS
Other wars are briefly described, but are not necessarily easy to fit into the timetable. For instance the four beasts of Daniel 7 will have a latter day as well as a historic significance and will be involved in a power struggle within the Mediterranean area, perhaps as part of the Beast's consolidation of his own power base. These are complex matters, major studies in their own right. Other nations, such as the King of the North and King of the South, will be in conflict later (Dan 11.40-44); we will look briefly at these in chapter 6, as we are fairly sure that they will be part of the build up to Armageddon.

We suspect that the earlier Trumpet judgments will begin to take effect in the latter part of the first three and a half years, but for reasons which we shall shortly give, we will leave the description of them until our next chapter. Every feature or sequence within the Day of Vengeance does not have to fit neatly into one half or the other; some overlap.

CHAPTER FIVE

The Great Tribulation

WHO IS AFFECTED?

In this chapter we will start at the half-way point of the Day of Vengeance, and continue to the immediate build-up to the battle of Armageddon. The Great Tribulation will be the more awesome half of the Day of Vengeance: "These are the days of vengeance, that all things which are written may be fulfilled" (Lk 21.22). This vengeance may be extended marginally beyond Christ's return to earth: "When the Lord Jesus is revealed from heaven with His mighty angels, in flaming fire taking vengeance on those who do not know God" (II Thess 1.7-8).

Isaiah writes: "For the indignation of the Lord is against all nations...It is the day of the Lord's vengeance, the year of recompense for the cause of Zion" (Isa 34.2, 8). For over two and a half thousand years Israel has had this assurance. For almost two thousand years the Church has been aware that the cause of Zion is not the only matter over which the Lord will execute His vengeance; but it is still one of them, and we must not forget this. The Year of Recompense is, of course, synonymous with the Year of the Lord's Redeemed.

Three groups will suffer during the Great Tribulation, though not for the same reasons:-

- The Tribulation saints
- Israel
- The unrepentant world

The Church will be with her Lord in Heaven. We will deal now very briefly with the Tribulation saints, a vast number of whom will be martyred. We have already seen them in Revelation chapter 7, and will learn a little more about them and how they are to suffer at the hands of the Beast. But once in Heaven, awaiting their resurrection bodies, they will be beyond all suffering. "They shall neither hunger any more nor thirst anymore; the sun shall not strike them, nor any heat; for the Lamb who is in the midst of the throne will shepherd them and lead them to living fountains of waters. And God will wipe away every tear from their eyes" (Rev 7.16-17).

The Great Tribulation has been predicted in prophecy as a time to be experienced by Israel just as frequently as has the Year of the Lord's Redeemed. A variety of names is used. We have seen how concerned Jesus was about its coming and how carefully He indicated a sure way of escape for those in Israel who would heed His warning at the appropriate time.

Dr Renald Showers says that the Septuagint translators use the same Greek word for 'distress' in the OT and 'trouble', as is found for 'tribulation' in the NT. "Alas! For that day is great, so that none is like it; and it is the time of Jacob's trouble, but he shall be saved out of it (Jer 30.7). Thus we could legitimately read, "It is the time of Israel's tribulation". Dr Showers adds: "The unparalleled time of trouble is identified with the Day of the Lord (Joel 2.1-2), the time of Jacob's trouble (Jer 30.7), and the Great Tribulation (Dan 12.1 and Matt 24.21). In light of this, and the fact that there can be only one unparalleled time of trouble, it can be concluded that the future Day of the Lord will include the same period as the time of Jacob's trouble and the Great Tribulation" (Your Tomorrow, Feb 1993). These terms all speak of the second 3½ years.

Later in the same article, Dr Showers adds: "Revelation 12.14 states that Israel will hide in the wilderness for a time, and times and half a time. Daniel 7.25 uses this same designation for the period during which the Antichrist will persecute the saints of the 70th week". We have up to this point thought of God's vengeance and wrath solely against the powers of evil and the lost. However it is noteworthy that of the forty-five mentions of vengeance in Scripture, not one describes God's vengeance upon His own. However there are many references to God's wrath upon His own in the Old Testament – wrath which is severe but not terminal. Speaking to the Jews, God said: "In My wrath I struck you, but in My favour I have had mercy on you" (Isa 60.10). In our sixth chapter we will encounter an exception – God's vengeance on Jews.

The third group of those who will suffer during the Great Tribulation are the unrepentant. We shall look at their suffering as we study the Trumpet and Bowl judgments later in this chapter.

THE MID-WAY POINT
We have already seen how, while there is no difficulty in predicting from Scripture much of what is to occur during these seven ominous years, fitting each event into the appropriate half is not always so easy. We dealt with the Gog and Magog invasion in the first half, because it *seems* to fit there. We will deal in this chapter with the Trumpet judgments because they pair very well with the Bowl judgments, which do fall entirely within the later half. There are still grey areas regarding the timing and we can return to them later. But, as we are about to see, there are also the most carefully confirmed timings of other events; these are of the greatest significance in God's final dealing with this world's rebelliousness.

What is established beyond all doubt is one *visible* key event which triggers others at the three and a half year point. We will explain the *invisible* one soon. The visible event is given the greatest prominence so must be examined. It is clearly the dividing point in Jesus' Olivet Discourse, a very specific sign to be watched for by the faithful in Israel in those dark days: We have already touched on it. "Therefore when you see the abomination of desolation, spoken of by Daniel the prophet, standing in the holy place (whoever reads, let him understand), then let those who are in Judea flee to the mountains" (Matt 24.15-16). Then follow instructions and advice for flight to safety, before the words: "For then there will be great tribulation, such as has not been seen since the beginning of the world until this time, no, nor ever shall be" (v.21). Jesus is totally forthright about this. It is not poetic language, neither is it exaggeration for effect. This is God the Son telling of a future time which will be worse than any time in this old world's history. Bible believing Christians cannot legitimately dismiss it, ignore it or explain it away. To say that it will not happen is a personal affront to God and defiance of the Bible as His revealed word.

Before we look further at this abomination, let us summarise all the other important things which are to happen at this mid-point or to follow on as the direct result. Several we have already encountered; others we have yet to enlarge upon. Simply listing them without comment may help us to see connections.

- Satan will be cast out of Heaven with many of his angels, having great wrath. (Rev 12.9)
- A Satanic trinity of evil will become evident – The Dragon, The Beast and the second beast or False Prophet (Rev 13.1-12).
- The Beast will break His seven year covenant with Israel (Dan 9.27).
- The Beast will set up the Abomination of Desolation in the Jerusalem Temple.
- The Beast will dismiss his religious mistress, Mystery Babylon, and demand personal worship from all, Satan himself will thus receive worship (II Thess 2.4, Rev 13.4).
- The Beast, having previously been head of his own realm, the Revived Roman Empire, will assume world-wide authority, except over true believers (Rev 13.8).
- Satan, the Dragon, will pursue and persecute all unprotected Jews (Rev 12.17).
- God will provide a refuge in the wilderness or desert for all believing Jews who heed His warning in time (Matt 14.16, Rev 12.6).
- The Beast may be slain, and resurrected by Satan (Rev 13.3). There is some doubt as to whether this verse applies to the Beast personally.

Rather than asking why the Beast chooses to break his covenant with the Jews at this point, we should ask why it is at this point he chooses to break his covenant. There is a subtle difference. But on closer examination we again find that it is the action of God which truly determines timing. It is God who expels Satan, and everything else follows in quick succession.

The one thing we do not believe is to happen at the mid-point is the Rapture. We mention this because of a small group known as Mid-Tribulation Rapturists. The Olivet Discourse is centred upon Jerusalem from the outset. Were the Church not to be caught up to Heaven until the mid-point, we would expect it to feature prominently during the Beginning of Sorrows, which it most certainly does not; moreover we would not expect to find Jewish evangelists sealed until after the Abomination.

SATAN'S EXPULSION

This event will be invisible on earth, though having enormous bearing upon it. Satan's future expulsion from Heaven is difficult to grasp, because one does not naturally associate the Devil with Heaven. It was Christ who created him (Col 1.16) "perfect in all his ways" (Ezek 28.15) and Christ who will destroy him. Before the creation of this world he was removed from his supreme angelic office of anointed covering cherub (Ezek 28.14), but he was not denied further access to Heaven. Throughout history he has been the malignant accuser of the brethren; we find him engaged in this activity as far back as Job, four thousand years ago, ranging the earth to bring before God hostile evidence against believers (Job 1.6-7, Rev 12.10). At times we find him in conflict with God's unfallen holy angels, his chief adversary being Michael, the Archangel, "the great prince who stands watch over the sons of your people" (Dan 12.1 and Jude 1.19). In Jude we learn that Michael still recognised certain rights and privileges in his angelic adversary, whom Paul calls the prince of the power of the air (Eph 2.2). Satan's subordinate fallen angels are in conflict with God's holy angels.

We have a rare insight in Dan 10.12-14, where the angelic prince, who is delegated by Satan with responsibility for Persia, delays for three weeks an answer to the prophet's prayer; this angelic being is evidently still active in Iran. In both these Daniel passages Satan and his deputy are engaged in conflict against Israel. In Revelation they are seen at the same old activity. At neither time was the Church on the scene, but we know that Satan has for the past nearly two thousand years been accusing Christians before God; this should be solemn and even embarrassing for us, because we often give him grounds. Jesus in His High Priestly role always has an answer for him, but that is thanks to Him and not to us. Satan's fate has been sealed since Jesus' crucifixion (Col 2.15), but he still seeks to devour.

However we are now looking at a time when the Church, being in glory, will be beyond any further accusation. John records: "So the great dragon was cast out, that serpent of old, called the Devil and Satan, who deceives the whole world; he was cast to the earth, and his angels were cast out with him...'Woe to the inhabitants of the earth and the sea! For the devil has come down to you, having great wrath, because he has a short time'" (Rev 12.9 & 12).

Satan has been attacking God's people since Eden; but the foreshortening of his time seems already to be leading to the shortening of his temper. We believe that he particularly hates the preaching and teaching of his coming vanquishment. It hurts his gigantic pride. Those of us involved in prophetic witness sometimes feel the pressure and must ever hide beneath the blood of the Lamb. Prophecy foretells his fate, and this he hates.

We know how short a time will then remain to him, a mere three and a half earthly years. His first priority is to pursue the "woman who gave birth to the male Child" (Rev 12.13). This is a reference back to the earlier part of Revelation 12. The woman there, with the sun and moon beneath her feet and crowned with twelve stars, is Israel, identified from Genesis 37.9. He immediately launches into a relentless persecution of her and her seed, knowing that if he can destroy Israel, the remaining prophecies against him will be void.

The woman of Revelation 12 cannot possibly be Mary, who will be safely in Heaven, risen with the remainder of the Church and beyond any assault by the Dragon. The symbolic representation of Mary in this likeness in Strasbourg Cathedral and elsewhere, espoused by the European Community hierarchy, is based on pagan concepts. Miracles unprecedented and unnecessary in the Church Age will be required at this dreadful time. Somehow, and we can do no more than guess at the details, believing Jews who heed Jesus' warning in His Olivet Discourse will be provided with means of flight, "two wings of a great eagle", and a safe refuge in the desert for three and a half years (Rev 12.14). Any God-fearing people who at that point have not fled, must flee without going home for any possessions, so immediate will the threat be. This provision seems to be limited only to those Jews resident in the Holy Land and will apparently be open only very briefly; those who miss it will live through that final holocaust. No doubt other Jews world-wide will suffer; and God's angels will be busy preserving them from total annihilation, because enough will survive to be recalled by angels when the Lord returns (Isa 5.26, Jer 16.14, Ezek 36.24, etc).

In Isa 26.20 we encounter one of God's most tender promises to Israel in her time of adversity: "Come, My people, enter your chambers, and shut your doors behind you; hide yourself, as it were, for a little moment, until the indignation is past. For behold the Lord comes out of His place to punish the inhabitants of the earth for their iniquity; the earth will also disclose her blood, and will no more cover her slain." What a blessing the obedient will derive from heeding the Lord's Olivet Discourse warning to flee! What tragedy and suffering will await those who hesitate! This Isaiah verse may *illustrate* the Rapture as the latter day Ark of refuge for the entire Church. But it applies directly and primarily to believers in Israel at the outset of the Great Tribulation.

THE TRINITY OF EVIL

Now at this juncture the Beast will have been leader of the Revived Roman Empire for around three and a half years. He is probably alive somewhere today and being groomed in the deepest occult mysteries, awaiting his opportunity. We have been referring to him as the Beast, but it is only from this point in Revelation 13 that this title is used in the Bible.

In verses 1 to 3 we learn more of the political heritage of the Beast, whom John sees rising from the sea. In Revelation 17, where the Beast is seen in his relationship with the religious harlot, the waters are shown to represent "peoples, multitudes, nations and tongues" (v.15), a truly trans-national setting; this suggests that he is a Gentile. For reasons which we gave in the third chapter, he could turn out to be a prince of the apostate church or even a prince of Islam – more likely the former, we think. He is shown to share the features of the first three Gentile empires listed in Daniel 2 as parts of the image, but which in Daniel 7 are likened to wild animals. Thus, in addition to his own Roman characteristics, he has something in his background and character of the lion, the bear and the leopard, or Babylon, Persia and Greece. He is to be the final head in a long succession of rulers going back to the late 7th Century BC. Throughout this time the beasts and sections of the image have described at various times both the empires and their emperors, as in Dan 2.37 et seq. As an individual this Beast is seen as the final head of the final empire (Rev 17.10). Some think that the sea referred to is the Mediterranean, rather than representing the nations – they may be right.

Opinions are divided as to whether Rev 13.3 & 13, which describes one of the Beast's heads being mortally wounded and miraculously healed, refers to the individual or to his empire. Is it that the Roman Empire is to be marvellously resurrected from its death bed, or is the individual to be slain and physically raised from the dead as Satan's mimicry of Jesus Christ? We already know from Daniel that the Roman Empire is to be revived in the last days. It may be only at the end of the first three and a half years that it will achieve the level of glory and dominance which it enjoyed two thousand years ago. Such commentators as varied as Alford, Baines and Walvoord maintain that the resurrection miracle is to occur with the state and not with the man; but equally respected authorities prefer the alternative interpretation. It seems to us from v.15 more likely that, because the image is to be of the mortally wounded but healed Beast, the reference is to the individual.

One of these interpretations should prove to be the correct one. For the Tribulation saints who witness it, this is likely to be an immensely important and unambiguous prophecy, yet another of God's ways of reassuring them that all is on course to fulfil His plans and to rescue them – "He who endures to the end shall be saved" (Matt 24.13). Iranian religious leaders tell us that the Mahdi is to be resurrected from a well where he has been waiting for over a thousand years to lead his victorious campaign, and that Jesus Christ will be his servant!! Could this be significant? It is certainly blasphemous.

It has been suggested, on the assumption that this is an individual, that the Beast will turn out to be the resurrected Judas, Nero, Napoleon, Hitler and so on. Judas Iscariot at least shares his title of Son of Perdition with the Beast, and there has been a recent much publicised attempt to rehabilitate "poor, misunderstood, misrepresented Judas". Walvoord points out that the sheer variety of suggestions put forward without any collateral confirmation detract from any of these suggestions being the correct interpretation. Another problem with the Judas theory is that his role would be more in keeping with the second beast than the first, and there is no hint that the second one is to be slain and resurrected.

All the world except God's elect will worship the Dragon and his Beast (v.4). He is to be allowed to continue in office for only forty-two months (v.5). Here are the first two persons of the trinity of evil being worshipped world-wide in the same way as we worship the Father and the Son. No doubt part of the deception noted in Matthew 24 and II Thessalonians 2 will be a campaign telling the world what a raw deal

Satan has had in the past and what a fine fellow he really is. A sizeable minority is already converted to this damnable view, while others follow him because they deliberately choose what they know to be evil. Dicing with death for 'kicks' is a popular modern pastime. But this is dicing with eternal death.

This adulation is something which Satan long ago offered Jesus in the temptation in the wilderness: "All this authority I will give You, and their glory; for this has been delivered to me, and I will give it to whomever I wish" (Lk 4.6). One wonders whether more blasphemous words have ever been uttered before and since creation. Throughout history Satan has delegated this authority at least in part to individuals whom we would describe as satanic monsters. But he has been saving up for his final fling with the most evil monster of them all. One of the best known of these prototypes was Antiochus Epiphanes, who, in the 2nd Century BC set up a blasphemous abomination in Jerusalem, and who was foretold in Dan 8.7 & 11 as a forerunner of the latter day Beast. That prophecy was immensely important for the faithful in the days of its first fulfilment. However we noticed earlier that the Gospel writer made it clear that an understanding was not to be limited only to contemporary generations (Matt 24.15).

"All who dwell on the earth will worship him, whose names have not been written in the Book of Life of the Lamb" (Rev 13.8). This is no election to damnation or salvation; it is the righteous act of God who knows the beginning from the end and who sees everything. Daniel writes: "He shall exalt and magnify himself above every god, shall speak blasphemies against the God of gods, and shall prosper till the wrath has been accomplished; for what has been determined shall be done. He shall regard neither the God of his fathers nor the desire of woman, nor regard any god; for he shall exalt himself above them all" (Dan 11.36-37). We are reminded here of how and why he will destroy Mystery Babylon, once he has made use of her for his purposes and feels powerful enough. Satan has been happy enough in the past to receive indirect worship from apostate religion and idolatry, and from the diversion of worship away from God. But now he will covet it for himself personally and will be prepared to dispense with all those intermediaries which have served him well for thousands of years.

THE FALSE PROPHET
Then we are introduced to the third person of the evil trio, the False

Prophet (Rev 13.11-18). He is said to rise from the earth or land. This suggests THE Land, namely the Promised Land, and that he, rather than the First Beast, must therefore be Jewish. It is virtually certain that one beast or the other must be Jewish in order to be accepted, and the second seems to be the stronger contender. Jesus said: "I have come in My Father's name, and you do not receive Me; if another comes in his own name, him you will receive" (Jn 5.43). He might possibly be half Jewish and half Edomite, sharing both sides of Isaac's descendants and acceptable to both Jew and Muslim. Both venerate prophets. Could it possibly be that he will produce credentials and claim to be both the awaited Jewish Messiah and the similarly awaited Islamic Twelfth Imam or Mahdi? This may sound preposterous, but it would be a master stroke on Satan's part and be almost universally applauded. We will not pursue this line of enquiry further, but it is worth bearing the possibility in mind.

His role *vis-à-vis* the First Beast within this devilish trinity is similar to that of the Holy Spirit to God the Son within the Holy Trinity. The Holy Spirit upholds and bears witness to Jesus Christ; "When He, the Spirit of truth, has come, He will guide you into all truth, for He will not speak on His own authority, but whatever He hears He will speak, and He will tell you things to come. He will glorify Me, for He will take of what is Mine and declare it to you" (Jn 16.13-14). What a blasphemous parody is going to be enacted during those forty-two months, by the one who will guide into all untruth!

The Second Beast or False Prophet is the one who "causes the earth and those who dwell in it to worship the first beast" (Rev 13.12). He is to have the greatest miraculous powers ever possessed by evil. His ability to deceive is going to be quite incredible. Even today we must exercise the greatest caution when we encounter what appears to be spectacular but questionable. Praying in the name of Jesus, claiming shelter under the blood of Calvary, has already exposed many a minor deceiver. But in the Great Tribulation it will be deception *par excellence*. Surviving believers "overcame him by the blood of the Lamb" (Rev 12.11).

The main roles of the two beasts are clearly defined, but there are what are at present puzzling perceived overlaps. A credibility with Muslims, Jews and apostate Christians would help to explain a lot. Babylon's prominent part in latter day events is suggestive. It partly depends upon whether Babylon's predicted desolation status applies to all history or just to the coming Millennium. Such passages as Jeremiah 50 and 51, where the Lord has a "time of vengeance" in store for her (51.6), seem to have a comprehensive future significance as well as a historical one. Certainly the late Saddam Hussein aspired to rebuild and re-instate this accursed city, which to date has been anathema to the Jews, among others. Revelation chapters 17 and 18 reveal both religious and commercial latter day roles for Babylon. We must ever be alert to developments in Iraq, especially should there be any realignment of borders and a separation of the northern formerly Assyrian area around Mosul (formerly Nineveh) from the more southern formerly Babylonian area around Baghdad.

On the other hand, for centuries Mystery Babylon has been readily identified with Rome, the apostate church which has been responsible, through the Inquisition and by other means, for the death of millions. Many of the pagan teachings, mysteries and practices which were absorbed by Rome, both during and after its Imperial days, arrived from Pergamos, described in Rev 2.13 as the site of Satan's throne, which took over as the satanic capital after ancient Babylon's demise. John marvels "with great amazement" when Mystery Babylon is exposed in her true colours (Rev 17.6); so may we. The best advice might be to wait and see, even though it is from Heaven that we will see and be able to rejoice at her ultimate downfall; "Rejoice over her, O heaven, and you holy apostles and prophets, for God has avenged you on her!" (Rev 18.20). The correlation between Jerusalem, Rome and Babylon needs constantly to be monitored by students of prophecy. We cannot over-emphasise the fact that saints in crises at different points of history have been comforted and sustained by secondary applications of prophecies. This is a work of God the Holy Spirit; very wonderful it is.

From Daniel 9, Matthew 24, Mark 13 and II Thessalonians 2 we have already learned something of the mid-point erection of the Abomination of Desolation in the Jerusalem Temple. The word 'abomination' implies that detestable thing which incurs God's wrath. From Rev 13 we learn that the Abomination will take the form of a fabulous and miraculous image of the Beast, and that it will be the False Prophet who will act in a priestly role, directing obeisance to the image, the Beast and the empire he heads.

It may very well transpire that the First Beast will remain in Jerusalem only long enough to receive spiritual recognition and worship, and will then return to Rome, the capital of his Revived Roman Empire or to Babylon as a world centre, and that the Second Beast or False Prophet will remain in Jerusalem as high priest of the temple and director of worship to the First Beast's image or Abomination of Desolation.

THE MARK OF THE BEAST

It is curious how many people have heard of the Four Horsemen of the Apocalypse, the Mark of the Beast and the Battle of Armageddon, who do not know that they must be born again or that Jesus died for their sins. Repentance has no appeal for the intransigent. However perhaps there are people alive today who will one day be challenged by the 666 identification of the lethal Mark of the Beast, and who may be warned by God's witnesses to repent or suffer the inevitable eternal damnation which follows acceptance of the Mark. It seems that all will somehow be warned of the dangers. "And the smoke of their torment ascends forever and ever; and they have no rest day or night, who worship the beast and his image, and whoever received the mark of his name (Rev 14.11).

It is not so much the number which damns eternally; it is the consequent worship of and allegiance to Satan's Beast which will incur God's wrath and put people beyond repentance and therefore salvation. In my early teens, nearly sixty years ago, I read in my parents' prophetic magazine of the Mark of the Beast and how it might apply. That was long before the age of embedded micro-chips and even more advanced technology, which now make it so very feasible to have a tiny device in the forehead or right hand without which a person may not buy or sell. But these devout writers of a previous generation believed that somehow these facts were going to materialise, simply because the Bible said that they would. Perhaps we have forgotten the extraordinary insight given to the prophets of old who, despite having no scientific knowledge, anticipated the cyber age. We should follow their example by accepting the obvious meanings of prophecy, rather than quibbling over prophecies where we do not yet understand the ways and means of their fulfilment. The significance of the number 666 will be clear to believers at the time.

The Mark of the Beast, which we assume will be visible to all, as it evidently was to John, will enable God's elect to be readily identified by its absence. So not only will they risk starvation through being unable to buy food; they will also, like marked Jews in Nazi Germany, become targets for persecution, pillaging and much more. The Beast's forty-two month authority includes making war with and overcoming the saints (Rev 13.7). "He shall speak pompous words against the Most High (and) shall persecute the saints of the Most High" (Dan 7.25). This helps to explain the huge number of Tribulation martyrs. The Gentile converts are not going to share the desert refuge with the faithful of Israel; there is no such provision described for them.

Why will God allow this killing? Perhaps it is because He does not want His own to endure the coming Wrath of God in the form of the Bowl judgments. It is difficult for us to grasp how much more blessed it will be to be one of Christ's martyrs than to survive in a totally alien world, swarming with Satan's agents, both human and demonic, when earth's harvest is being reaped. Those who like to place the Rapture at the end of the Great Tribulation (Post-Tribulationists) would find a remarkably small Church, if a Church at all, left to take part! They also have a job explaining the central role played by Israel throughout the seven years, when, according to them, the Church will still be on earth.

COMPARING TRUMPET AND BOWL JUDGMENTS

Jesus gave us a simple but straightforward overview of Daniel's final week of years in His Olivet Discourse, especially as recorded in Matthew and Mark. For convenience we are dealing with all of the Trumpets in this chapter, being fairly confident, as we have stated, that the effect of the first four Trumpet judgments will be felt on earth within the latter part of the Beginning of Sorrows. The last three trumpets are described as woes, by an angel flying through the heavens (Rev 8.13). The fifth Trumpet or first Woe seems to bring us to the momentous events of the mid-point. As we said at the beginning of the last chapter, when these events take place, the wise shall understand. What God has already clearly revealed to us is the sequence of each series; we learn much thereby.

The Trumpets and Bowls are alike in many respects except in intensity and geographical coverage. The following table is taken from Volume 6 of J Sidlow Baxter's, Explore The Book.

vii, ix SEVEN TRUMPETS	SEVEN VIALS (BOWLS)
1. On the earth	1. On the earth
2. On the sea	2. On the sea
3. On the rivers	3. On the rivers
4. Sun, moon stars	4. Sun
5. Darkness, scourge	5. Darkness, scourge
6. Euphrates: army	6. Euphrates: kings
7. "Nations angry" "Wrath"; "Great voices"; "Time no longer"	7. "Nations fell" "Wrath"; "Voices"; "Thunderings"; "It is done"
x, xi Parenthetical: Jerusalem in the Great Tribulation	Parenthetical (xvii-xviii); Babylon in the Wrath of God
xi;15 End of seventh trumpet "Kingdom of the Lord" The 24 elders worship "Wrath" to come	After seventh vial (xix) "Lord God reigneth" The 24 elders worship "Armageddon"

We feel that Dr Baxter has taken slight liberties in making the first and fifth Trumpets and first and fifth Bowls appear to correspond. Nevertheless there are many similarities in the way in which the two sets of judgments progress. The perceived break between the Trumpets and Bowls is a parenthesis to introduce important personalities and events apart from the three main judgment series. It does not necessarily indicate a break in continuity.

Some of the Bowls are explicitly described as being three times as disastrous as the Trumpets, and they occur in very quick succession. We explained back in our third chapter the problems of putting the Seals, Trumpets and Bowls end-to-end. They start at different points but all end with events around the Lord's return. The above table illustrates this with the Trumpets and Bowls, and a little later we will quote the description of the sixth Seal to confirm this 'coterminous' arrangement, first noticed by this writer in Dr EJ Miller's 'The Final Battle', and found still to be convincing after several years of contemplation.

THE TRUMPET JUDGMENTS

There is a significant pause while the angels stand by waiting to sound their trumpets. God's wrath is often incurred by direct attacks upon Him, in other words by blasphemy. But it may also be occasioned by attacks upon His redeemed, "He will avenge the blood of His servants" (Deut 32.43); "He will redeem their life from oppression and violence; and precious shall be their blood in His sight" (Ps 72.14). During the interval before they sound, it is revealed that the Trumpets are at least partly a response to the prayers of the saints, in other words those still on earth or perhaps those recently slain, awaiting in Heaven the resurrection of their bodies.

More than a hundred years ago TB Baines wrote: "Their prayers are presented before God by the angel, probably Christ Himself, with 'much incense'. The incense burnt on the golden altar at the time of prayer (Lk 1.10) symbolised the perfect acceptance of Christ giving efficacy to the people's petitions. So in this figurative scene. The altar stands before the throne, not here the mercy seat, but the throne of judgment; and from this golden altar of incense, the prayers of the remnant for deliverance and judgment rise to God, performed with all the fragrance of Christ, and draw down a speedy answer. As often in the Old Testament when He appeared to His servants of old, Jesus is described as an angel. In His priestly role here He stands between His Father and His people."

The nature of the first four judgments, before the three Woes commence, is largely environmental, and ominously like the disasters which men of science now fear could befall the earth if our present rate of squandering our natural resources and of polluting our environment is not curbed. How re-assuring it is that the God who nearly two thousand years ago foretold all this, also promised a time of glorious restoration upon earth afterwards. The Creator can remedy what would defeat all our scientists put together. How He will accomplish this is not our concern. Perhaps in our resurrection bodies we may possibly be apportioned a share in this rewarding work.

The first Trumpet involves the destruction of a third of all the trees and all of the grass; we may assume that the latter includes cereal crops. Trees take many years to regenerate, but the grass will have made some recovery by the time the fifth angel sounds. By then however the loss of livestock and foodstuffs will be incalculable. Trees absorb carbon dioxide. We suspect that the atmospheric balance will be disastrously distorted, and this may exacerbate the effect of the fourth Trumpet.

We have been conditioned to believe that our environment is all important, but our Creator's perspective and values are infinitely higher than ours. As at the time of the Flood, the human soul and spirit are worth more than all the forests and grasslands of the world put together. These latter are expendable and can and will be recreated or replenished in His good time. Yet, although it is God who authorises the Seals, Trumpets and Bowls, from His perspective it is not He who is destroying the world but men. In Revelation 11.18 we read: "The nations were angry, and Your wrath has come...You...should destroy those that destroy the earth". When Jesus said, in verses which we quoted earlier, that, but for these days being shortened, no flesh would be spared (Matt 24.22), we must take into consideration the potential destructiveness of future wars and man's present nuclear capability to destroy all life on this planet many times over. Even the Bowls will inflict less damage on the planet than mankind, unrestrained by God, could do when driven by demonic forces.

For over half a century we have had a nuclear stalemate. Nuclear weapons were possessed only by comparatively stable and responsible nations, who, while they used their power at times to their political advantage, at least did their best to maintain a policy of non-proliferation. They strove to keep the nuclear club small. I personally served as British Liaison Officer to Soviet forces in Germany at the height of the Cold War, and can bear witness to the albeit strained mutual respect that existed between West and East. The real fear was that a rogue government should acquire weapons of mass destruction, or that they should fall into the hands of a madman.

Recently, as is well known, a number of volatile Asian countries have come to the brink of possessing the ability to deliver such means. Much of the hardware and technology has been acquired from parts of the former Soviet empire via unscrupulous dealers. At the time of writing North Korea and Iran are latest to hit the headlines. Such is the posturing and bravado that it is not always possible to make an accurate assessment. One assumes exaggeration, but does not underestimate the dangers.

What John saw when the second and third Trumpets sounded was what appeared to be a huge meteorite and an asteroid strike. We have no authority to say which of these, if either, is the correct interpretation, but the descriptions are remarkably in keeping with what scientists tell us has happened with major meteorite strikes in the past or would happen with the impact of an asteroid. Rogue asteroids are now seen as a genuine threat. With one Trumpet we see "something like a great mountain burning with fire" and with the other "a great star burning like a torch" falling from heaven. The one leads to the destruction of a third of marine life, suggesting a landing in the sea, and the other a land strike, leading to a third of the rivers and fresh water lakes being lethally polluted. It was the popular press rather than the mainstream church which publicised the fact that Rev 8.11 calls the star "wormwood", and that Chernobyl is the name of a variety of wormwood. The Greek *sinthos* means both wormwood and undrinkable. Perhaps there was no significance in Chernobyl, but Christians have no right whatsoever to be scathing, as many were when the secular world was enquiring about the signs of the times. Perhaps God in His mercy was allowing a warning message to go out to the world, despite growing obtuseness in the Church.

The fourth Trumpet will hit the atmosphere, resulting in the light of the sun and of the moon being reduced by a third. We cannot be sure whether the one third is spread over the entire world or is localised to a single area, such as the Beast's home domain. Perhaps the answer lies somewhere between. One would not expect a sharp line of demarcation. However there is a minor precedent, in that some of the plagues with which God struck Pharaoh in Moses' day did not affect the area of Goshen, where most of the Children of Israel were concentrated (Ex 8.22 etc). God is still well able to safeguard His own and to target whom He chooses.

There is every indication that, when the Bowls of Wrath are poured out, almost at the culmination of the Great Tribulation, the way to the Mercy Seat and forgiveness leading to salvation will finally be closed (Rev 15.8). But before that, during the earlier Trumpet judgments, the Gospel will still be preached. These will be drastic measures to encourage repentance when all else has failed. For the first time in human history as far as we know an angel is to preach salvation. One is seen "flying in the midst of heaven, having the everlasting gospel to preach to those who dwell on earth – to every nation, tribe, tongue and people – saying with a loud voice, 'Fear God and give glory to Him, for the hour of His judgment has come; and worship Him who made heaven and earth, the sea and springs of water'" (Rev 14.7). Exactly how this will appear we are not told, but it will apparently be unambiguous and effective for those inclined to pay attention. It will be at that critical juncture that the Beast will make his exclusive demand for all human worship. The temporal consequences of refusing the one will be awesome; the eternal consequence of the other will be indescribable.

THE THREE WOES

Woes, as we have seen, are the names given to the final three Trumpet judgments. This time the impact will not be chiefly environmental, and they are therefore more difficult to comprehend.

The fifth Trumpet or first Woe is to reveal a mass release of demons from the Abyss. This will, we feel, be timed to coincide with Satan's expulsion from Heaven. Fallen angels come into two categories; we are not told of the comparative size of the groups. Numerous demons have been on earth, presumably since the Fall of man in Eden, going about their master's occult business. It will be recalled that when Jesus cast the legion of demons out of a possessed man, they begged Him to allow them to enter into the swine (Matt 8.31). The pigs rushed down into the sea and were drowned; but possessing dead pigs was evidently preferable to the alternative which Jesus could have chosen, which was to send them to the Abyss or bottomless pit to await this brief latter day release.

However there are other demons who are so evil that they have been imprisoned in the Abyss since either before the Creation or since the Flood; probably the latter. Peter says that they are in chains of darkness awaiting a future judgment (II Pet 2.4). From Rev 9.1 it seems that one of God's angels is to be directed to give the expelled Satan the key to release these evil reinforcements from the Pit. Whether people will be conscious of this we do not know, but John saw them pouring forth to wreak havoc upon the earth for five short months, and people will most certainly feel the effects. We are not told whether they will be returned to the Abyss after this period or be allowed to remain active until the Lord returns. They will be headed by the only named fallen angel other than Satan himself, Apollyon, the destroyer.

They are described by John in Rev 9.3-9. Such is their dreadful appearance, that we feel that it is just as well that we are not normally allowed to see the world of the unclothed spirits. At least as Christians we would be given the same assurance as Elisha's servant, whose eyes were specially opened to see the heavenly horses and chariots of fire around his master, and to know that "those who are with us are more than those who are with them" (II Kings 6.16-17). These demons are to have massive powers, but will not be authorised to kill anyone. Unrepentant mankind will have to contend with unseen enemies who can inflict the most appalling physical pain, to the point where they will seek death, but be unable to find it.

It is reassuring to know that satanic power is not limitless. The Egyptian sorcerers were able to replicate some of the plagues. But they were soon outclassed by Moses and had to concede "this is the finger of God" (Ex 8.19). Depraved human actions together with Satan's fury will undoubtedly add to the misery during the Great Tribulation; but the judgments will be unmistakably the finger of God.

The sixth Trumpet or second Woe concerns the River Euphrates, as does the sixth Bowl. But whereas the sixth Bowl judgment, as we shall shortly see, is very easily understood, the sixth Trumpet is one of the more puzzling disclosures of Revelation. The fact that it is foretold in Rev 9.20-21 that nobody is to repent as the result of this Woe is an indication of a late date. Firstly we learn of four angels bound at the River Euphrates (Rev 9.14). For how long they have been bound we are not told – probably since ancient times. Barnhouse thinks that they are holy angels with a sort of exalted sentry duty on this border. The Euphrates is firstly considered to be the traditional demarcation line between East and West, secondly the eastern boundary of the land promised to Israel, and thirdly the furthest limit of the ancient Roman Empire, and perhaps of the Beast's domain. So it is of significance to both God and Satan. Most other commentators see these angels as evil, connected with ancient Babylon.

These angels are released, having power to kill a third of mankind (v.18). We are also told of a two hundred million strong army. Such is the description, that it is not clear whether these are demonic or human warriors. They sound like creatures from science fiction, with killing power both in their mouths and in their tails. However, when we remember that nineteen centuries of believers have had to make some sense of this passage, it is perhaps not surprising that the vision of this immense latter day fighting force should have been depicted in a way which was frightening and manifestly evil, without being fully comprehensible. In view of the fact that the fifth Trumpet revealed a demonic force emerging from a known source, it seems much more likely that the sixth is a description of something human - the huge invasion force, which will march from the Orient before Armageddon (16.12). Therefore it seems wise to leave further comment until we see the build up to Armageddon early in our next chapter.

The final Trumpet and Woe is not recorded until various other matters have been dealt with, and seven thunders, whose messages have been withheld from us, have sounded. However we meet the angel with the seventh Trumpet just before he sounds (Rev 10.7), when it is announced that "the mystery of God would be finished, as He declared to His servants the prophets". This mystery cannot be the Church as some have suggested, because that was never declared to the prophets. The Old Testament prophets' view revealed in the middle ground of their vision, as it were, the Lord's First Coming, and in the distance the Great Tribulation, followed at an even greater distance by the Year of the Lord's Redeemed. Their perspective did not allow them to distinguish between middle ground and distance. The Church was out of their sight in a wide valley. It should be very much easier for us, who can see the First Coming and Church Age in retrospect, to distinguish between First and Second Coming prophecies.

What was revealed, however, was God's ultimate triumph over evil, a theme which recurs time and again in Old Testament prophecy, but which has not happened during the Church Age. Only when the Bowls are fully poured out will this be achieved. Thus, by the time the seventh Trumpet angel does sound, heavenly voices will be able to proclaim: "The kingdoms of this world have become the kingdoms of our Lord and of His Christ, and He shall reign forever and ever" (11.15); thus we are transported beyond Armageddon and beyond the theme of our chapter. However we might pause to ask why this is described as a Woe. Surely it is because Christ's victory is the utter defeat of His enemies on earth. While it will be immensely joyful for some, it will be incredibly woeful for the unrepentant.

THE BOWLS OF WRATH

The Authorised Version uses the unfamiliar term 'vial', but the Revised, Darby and most if not all modern versions say 'bowl'. Emptying out a bowl of God's wrath is immensely descriptive, if terrifying.

At last we are coming to the climax of the ages. Old as well as New Testament prophecies point to this time which simply has to come; it is demanded by God's holiness and righteousness. It is demanded as a response to those who have been victims of evil. We quote three well known OT prophecies.

"Behold, the day of the Lord comes, cruel with both wrath and fierce anger, to lay land desolate; and He will destroy its sinners from it. For the stars of heaven and their constellations will not give their light; the sun will be darkened in its going forth, and the moon will not cause its light to shine. I will punish the world for its evil, and the wicked for their iniquity...Therefore I will shake the heaven, and the earth will move out of her place, in the wrath of the Lord of Hosts and in the day of His fierce anger" (from Isa 13.9-13).

"The earth is violently broken, the earth is split open, the earth is shaken exceedingly, the earth shall reel to and fro like a drunkard, and shall totter like a hut...It shall come to pass in that day that the Lord will punish on high the hosts of the exalted ones, and on earth the kings of the earth...then the moon will be disgraced and the sun ashamed" (Isa 24.19-23).

"Alas! For that day is great, so that none is like it; and it is the time of Jacob's trouble, but he shall be saved out of it" (Jer 30.7). But what final comfort is assured to God's own following this awful time. A few verses later we read that promise of God which leaves Replacement Theology in tatters: "Though I make a full end of all nations where I have scattered you, yet will I not make a complete end of you. But I will correct you in justice, and I will not let you go altogether unpunished" (v.11). God has never made a full end of these nations to date, so the promise of fulfilment still stands. However much we love Israel, we must bear in mind that she has yet to undergo more divine punishment before restoration.

Just as the Trumpets will not be allowed to sound until certain steps have been taken in Heaven, so the Bowls will not be poured out until other steps are taken in Heaven. In Revelation 14 and 15 we find the heavenly background to the Bowls of Wrath – the final plagues before the return of Jesus. In 14.14-16 we encounter an angel apparently instructing Christ: "Thrust in Your sickle and reap, for the time has come for You to reap, for the harvest of the world is ripe." Dr Walvoord says: "It is remarkable that an angel should thus address the Son of Man, but it should be regarded as an entreaty of a holy angel to Christ as the Son of Man in His position as Judge of men (cf Jn 5.22,27)." (The Revelation of Jesus Christ, A Commentary). In such a manner the Psalmist often addresses God, seeking vengeance; it is always a plea, never a command. This desire of saints and angels for this evil age to be wound up and its perpetrators to be judged appears again and again in Revelation.

Then the seven angels with the Bowls or last plagues appear, but before we see the Bowls being poured out, we have another double glimpse into Heaven to see more saints and the heavenly temple or tabernacle.

In Hebrews 8 we read: "We have such a High Priest, who is seated at the right hand of the throne of the Majesty in the heavens, a Minister of the sanctuary and of the true tabernacle which the Lord erected, and not man...On earth...there are priests...who serve the copy and shadow of the heavenly things as Moses was divinely instructed when he was about to make the tabernacle" (vv.1-5 with Ex 25.40). It was the heavenly tabernacle where Jesus, whilst His body still hung on the cross under the blanket of the dark, "with His own blood entered the Most Holy place once for all" (Heb 9.12). This is how and why He was able to cry: "It is finished!" (Jn 19.30). Just as the Seals and Trumpets emanated from the authority and actions of the once slain Lamb of God, so the heavenly Temple, where His blood still avails, is central to pouring out of the ensuing Bowls of Wrath.

The first Bowl brings about a great pandemic to all except believers, inflicting "loathsome sores" upon all (Rev 16:2). This plague is particularly linked with the worship of the Beast. From verse 11 we learn that this is not to be a short sharp shock; the sores will be unrelieved during the fifth Bowl. The second and third Bowls are poured out upon the sea and rivers respectively, the same targets as the second and third Trumpets. But now no mention is made of any celestial bodies landing on the earth; this might be an extension of these trumpets or might not; but what we are told is that this time they will be world-wide. All marine and freshwater life will perish. God knows that that would happen anyway through nuclear and chemical action, were man's activities to continue unabated.

The fourth bowl, like the fourth Trumpet, affects the sun. However now, perhaps through the removal of protective atmospheric layers, it will beat down mercilessly to "scorch men with fire" (16.8) – global warming with a vengeance! At this stage the only reaction is blasphemy. The fifth Bowl brings darkness, but only to the Beast's kingdom. The sixth Bowl is selective, like some of the Trumpet judgments, in that it affects only the Beast's capital and realm: "His kingdom became full of darkness; and they gnawed their tongues because of the pain" (16.10). Such is the intensity of these Bowl judgments that it is clear that they must happen in quick succession if human life is to survive them.

The seventh Bowl takes us to the great summons to the battle of Armageddon and is probably the most dramatic of all the judgments. However we will leave this until our next chapter.

CHAPTER SIX

The Climax to The Day of Vengeance

ASSEMBLING FOR ARMAGEDDON

Two further things are to happen shortly before the Battle of Armageddon. Vast armies from the cardinal points of the compass are to muster and advance on the Holy Land, and Babylon the Great is to be destroyed. Putting all these cataclysmic events in order and working out the degree of overlap is outside our scope. Indeed, it would probably be impossible to get a perfect consensus even among Pre-Millennial scholars. We hope this summary will be helpful and informative within those limitations.

The collapse of Babylon the Great appears to be finalised as the seventh angel pours out his Bowl (Rev 16.17). The armies of the world will be converging on the Holy Land during the last days of Babylon, in the interval between the sixth and seventh Bowls. Such is the vast scale of the military deployments that, although many troops may be airlifted or travel by sea, the bulk of the forces must come overland, many of them travelling through some of the most difficult terrain on earth; this is bound to take months.

Much of the world is already totally dependent upon high technology, and is featured by ever widening separation of grower and consumer. This trend is hardly likely to reverse. As the Tribulation period draws to an end, except in those dwindling areas of subsistence economies, life will have become well nigh impossible because of the failure of transport networks, power stations, computer systems and fuel supplies, upon which modern society depends. Communication satellites are likely to have fallen out of orbit. The entire world will be starving or on the brink of starvation – in other words desperate.

Even the political genius of the Beast will be unable to find a solution; and in any case, he will be no benefactor, rather a destroyer, like his master.

As the sixth Bowl is poured out, John records: "And I saw three unclean spirits like frogs coming out of the mouth of the dragon, out of the mouth of the beast, and out of the mouth of the false prophet. For they are the spirits of demons, performing signs, which go out to the kings of the earth and of the whole world, to gather them to the battle of that great day of God Almighty...And they gathered them together to the place called in Hebrew, Armageddon" (Rev 16:13-14).

Commenting on this chapter, Charles C Ryrie says: "God is directing this (v.19); demons accomplish it by using earthly rulers (v.16); Satan, the Beast and the false prophet are involved in it (v.13); yet the kings of the earth will think they are making decisions of their own free will." (Revelation: New Edition). We read in Zeph 3.8: "My determination is to gather the nations to My assembly of kingdoms, to pour on them My indignation, all My fierce anger; all the earth shall be devoured with the fire of My jealousy."

Antichrist, in his role as ruler of the Revived Roman Empire, will not have things all his own way, though for part of the seven years he will have world-wide control. We may reasonably think of him as the King of the West (the direction of Rome relative to Israel), although Scripture only refers by title to Kings of the North, South and East. So used are we Christians to an awareness of the infinite divine love that exists within the Holy Trinity, that we may be tempted to assume subconsciously that within the unholy trinity of the Dragon and his two beasts there will at least be some respect and loyalty. However if we think a little more about it, we will realise that the three are united only in their detestation of the Holy Trinity and the saints. Presumably to Satan even his two latter day dupes will be expendable as their usefulness draws to an end and as their doom looms ever closer.

While the Kings of the East are slowly mustering their gargantuan forces, intense military activity will be taking place in and around the Middle East. The Kings of the North and South are last in a line of bitter rivalries that go back thousands of years to the rulers of Egypt, Syria and their hinterlands. Israel and its lesser neighbours, being buffer states, were frequently caught up in protracted campaigns. Daniel chapter 11.1-35 is largely a warning to Inter-Testament believers of conflicts between soon-to-appear Kings of the North and South, who were to take the form of the Ptolemaic and Seleucid quarters of the disintegrated empire of Alexander the Great. Very accurate these prophecies proved to be; what an encouragement they were to 2nd Century BC patriots, such as the Maccabees. But from 11.36 on Daniel's prophecy switches without warning to the Great Tribulation. This is confirmed by Dan 12.1 which starts with, "At that time" and goes straight into the unprecedented time of trouble. Moreover, reliable historians, who recount in detail all the events which are recorded in the earlier part of Daniel 11, have nothing to say about the verses from 36 to the end of the chapter. These can only be future.

The King of the North must not be confused with Gog, who comes from the *far* North. Daniel 11 is quite explicit in identifying the two quarters of the Greek empire after Alexander's death Both the geographical details and the fate of the King of the North are in complete contrast with Ezekiel's description of Gog. The North here means roughly Syria, Kurdistan and what now is the north-west half of Iraq; ancient borders frequently changed, so it is difficult to be precise.

Now verse 36 describes a king whose details match perfectly the First Beast, who will almost certainly have a garrison in Israel as part of his treaty following the Gog and Magog invasion and in support of the temple which he will think he has annexed as his own. Suddenly he is to be attacked by the King of the South and his allies (11.40); this is in turn to provoke the fury of the King of the North who will attack him in great strength, plundering Egypt and also occupying the ground between Jerusalem and the Mediterranean coast and part of Jerusalem (v.45). This explains some of the armies encountered in Zechariah chapters 12 and 14 in an area some sixty miles south of the military concentration at Armageddon.

Under the sixth Bowl we read: "Then the sixth angel poured out his bowl on the great River Euphrates, and its water was dried up, so that the way of the kings of the east might be prepared (Rev 16.12). This massive assembly, as we have seen, will be demon driven, albeit within the permissive will and plan of God. Aims, objectives and priorities will shift as they advance westward. Initially the motives may include some of those mentioned earlier, a desperate search for *lebensraum*, in a devastated world living far below subsistence level, with no prospect of recovery from a human standpoint. Enmity, rivalry, hatred and rebellion and ambition for world conquest will be futher motives. The desire to own the strategic and symbolic city of Jerusalem may also provide impetus, for there could be millions of Muslims in this mega-force, from Pakistan, Bangladesh, Indonesia, Malaysia etc, who may over the three previous years have had reservations about the worship of an image, traditionally abhorrent to Islam.

But it is within the sixth Trumpet that we are actually given the number of troops involved – two hundred million! (Rev 9.16). Interestingly this is precisely the number which some time ago China boasted she could put into the field. But we should note that it is not the 'King' but the 'Kings' of the East who are described - several nations rather than one. Even if the population of China declines as the result of the various judgments, some of the world's other most populous nations could also furnish many tens of millions. We accept the Bible's figure as being accurate. It was the sixth Trumpet which, as we saw earlier, released four angels bound at the Euphrates, who may somehow be instrumental in further facilitating the river crossing at what may be defended bridgeheads.

Eventually the initial aims and objectives of this international conflict will be forgotten. "The kings of the earth set themselves, and the rulers take counsel together, against the Lord and against His Anointed...He who sits in the heavens shall laugh; the Lord shall hold them in derision" (Ps 2.2-4). What incomprehensible ignorance and underestimation of God's power lies behind this challenge! Yet it will be a direct confrontation with the Creator Himself. Of course this is utter madness; but demon driven armies will no longer be controlled by common sense. "It is apparent that the satanic purpose is to gather all the military might of the world to contend against the armies from heaven. It turns out of course to be totally futile, but, as in other efforts of Satan, he is compelled by his very nature to do his best to stand in the way of God's conquest." (JF Walvoord, Major Bible Prophecies).

SITUATION REPORT AS AT ZERO HOUR MINUS ONE

A comprehensive situational report of the battle at the moment before Jesus' spectacular intervention is quite impossible at present. We have detailed reports from only one sector of the battle zone, namely Jerusalem and its approaches, plus information about the vast river crossing. But what do we know about Armageddon and *its* troop deployments?

The actual name 'Armageddon' means 'mountain of Megiddo' (*Har Meggiddo*). It occurs only once in the Bible, in Rev 16.16, quoted above, where it is identified as the place where the demons will concentrate the world's armies. The valley of Megiddo is an ancient battle site, once described by Napoleon as theoretically the ideal battleground for all the armies of the world. TB Baines writes: "Here it was that the most formidable Gentile oppressors were overthrown, when God arose for the deliverance of His people. Here it was that 'the kings came and fought...by the waters of Megiddo. They fought from heaven; the stars in their courses fought against Sisera.' (Judg 5.19-20). It is obvious how admirable a type this furnishes of the great battle yet to come." (The Revelation of Jesus Christ). There also Gideon defeated the Midianites and later Saul, Jonathan and Josiah were slain.

Why is the greater detail reserved in Scripture for the war in the Jerusalem sector? Why do we gain much more intelligence from the Old, rather than the New, Testament? Why is information about the international confrontation further north so limited in comparison? The answer is surely simple. We are told that Jesus' return to earth, fulfilling the promise made at His departure almost two thousand years ago, will be to the outskirts of Jerusalem, though he will also be seen in glorious wrath at Armageddon as he destroys the satanic hosts. There are warnings in the Olivet address for the Judean resident Jews at that time, because it is to their rescue that Jesus will come to Olivet, at the most critical juncture of all military history. Thus Jerusalem is our natural focal point, though from the point of view of routing His enemies, Armageddon will be central.

Thus we have the forces of the King of the North deployed around and partly in Jerusalem; but they will be beset by appalling difficulties. "'Behold I will make Jerusalem a cup of drunkenness to all the surrounding peoples, when they lay siege against Judah and Jerusalem...In that day,' says the Lord, 'I will strike every horse with confusion, and its rider with madness; I will open My eyes on the house of Judah, and will strike every horse of the people with blindness'" (Zech 12.2-4). Modern armour and missile systems are highly dependent upon electronics. Somehow God will ensure that such systems and their operators will be neutralised, incapacitated, blinded.

"In that day that I will seek to destroy all the nations that come against Jerusalem. And I will pour on the house of David and on the inhabitants of Jerusalem the Spirit of grace and supplication; then they will look on Me whom they pierced..." (Zech 12.9-10). This takes us right up to the Second Coming in Power. We are brought to the same glorious point in Zech 14.2-4: "I will gather all the nations to battle against Jerusalem; the city shall be taken, the houses rifled, and the women ravished. Half of the city shall go into captivity, but the remnant of the people shall not be cut off from the city. Then the Lord will go forth and fight against those nations as He fights in the day of battle. And in that day His feet shall stand on the Mount of Olives".

However we have a dichotomy here; an inviolable Jerusalem and a breached city. David Baron is helpful in clearing up this apparent problem: "The first verses of this fourteenth chapter, which are an expansion and amplification of the last three verses of the preceding chapter, lead us back, I believe, to the point of time with which the *twelfth* chapter opens, and tells us of the judgment which is first allowed of God to be inflicted on Jerusalem in the final siege..." (The Visions and Prophecies of Zechariah). Nor need we be surprised to find in this chapter (14) a partial reiteration of events which had already been announced by the prophet in chaps 12 and 13. This seems to be the more widely accepted view among Pre-Millennial writers. The impact of the Lord's coming as described in Zech 14 is thus much greater.

We rephrase our recent question because it is so important. If these stupendous events are taking place on the Jerusalem front, what is left to happen at Armageddon, which is generally regarded as the epicentre, as confirmed by Rev 16.16? The battle at Jerusalem concerns God's rescue of Israel, whereas at Armageddon He deals with those world forces which are challenging Him directly. So often in latter day prophecies regarding Israel there are two levels of oppression and antagonism, the local level with Arab neighbours and the truly international, 'United Nations level'. So it will be then. The Old Testament portrays the Second Coming with the emphasis on the world's challenge to God through enmity against Israel, Zechariah giving us the most concentrated coverage. Revelation emphasises the global aspects and the demonic challenge; the Olivet Discourse bridges the gap, but still with a Judean bias. All are equally valid.

As we have already seen, Jerusalem will have been caught up in the comparatively local confrontation of the Kings of the North and South; both have been virulently anti-Semitic down through the centuries. But the bulk of the world's armies are concentrating on Armageddon, bent on venting their fury on God Himself. It will be there that He will deal with Satan, the Beast and the False Prophet and their forces, human and demonic.

DESTRUCTION OF BABYLON THE GREAT
Babylon has ever been symbolic of rebellion against God. After the Flood God said to Noah and his sons: "Be fruitful and multiply, and fill the earth" (Gen 9.1). He initially allowed men and women a much longer lifespan than the later three score years and ten, so the population naturally expanded rapidly. However very soon, in defiance of God's command, they said to each other: "Come, let us build ourselves a city, and a tower whose top is in the heavens; let us make a name for ourselves, lest we be scattered abroad over the face of the whole earth" (Gen 11.4). Instead of exercising the faith of their forefather, Noah, they embraced the old astrology which had probably been passed down to them from the old cursed world by Ham. They proceeded to build an abomination, a ziggurat, which

led to God's wrath and their consequent confusion and dispersal. Such was Babylon's birth.

We have already seen how, probably early in the Great Tribulation, Satan's Beast will, when it has served his purpose, destroy the age old religious part of Babylon – the ultimate form of mystery religion which has beguiled the world for so long. At the close of the Great Tribulation will occur the destruction of Babylon the Great, the final commercial monstrosity, devoid of the last elements of honesty and respectability since the departure Heaven-wards of the Church. The entire structure, totally given over to greed, corruption, the worship of mammon, with its huge infrastructure of electronics, power supply, communications and transport, will not so much grind to a halt as the result of the Trumpet and Bowl judgments, as disintegrate: "Alas, alas that great city Babylon, that mighty city! For in one hour your judgment has come" (Rev 18.10). The whole rotten structure will disintegrate as completely as the Tower of Babel.

"Great Babylon was remembered before God, to give her the cup of the wine of the fierceness of His wrath" (16.19). Whether this rebuilding on the old site on the Plain of Shinar in modern Iraq is before or after the Rapture, is not the most important question; it is what it stands for that matters. Certainly there would be great appeal for "third world" nations for a world commercial centre away from the United States with its Western capitalism and its Christian associations. A new expanded grandiose world trade centre could very quickly appear there. A decade ago an enterprising Malaysian government built a magnificent trade centre on the island of Labuan, ready to take over the commercial role of Hong Kong should China have closed its commercial activities. In the event it was not required and Malaysia was left with a white elephant. Babylon could feasibly and speedily replace London, New York, Frankfurt, Tokyo and much more. This of course is speculation, but it would tie in with Revelation 18.

Revelation 18 describes the dreadful moral state of this monstrosity, which will have become dominated by demonic forces (v.2) and will have corrupted all world rulers. The traded commodities, familiar to 1st and 2nd Century believers, can be up-dated with a little imagination to stocks shares and all the other paraphernalia of the modern Vanity Fair, which will even include trading in men's souls (v.13). The heavenly reaction, found in the opening verses of Revelation 19, is one of rejoicing, devoid of regret. The fall of Babylon the Great is accompanied by the mother of all earthquakes. It is all too easy for us, so involved in the world, to be like Lot's wife and mourn the loss of these institutions. But at that time we will have no regrets whatsoever. A spell in Heaven will have rectified our attitudes.

CATACLYSMIC SIGNS AND EVENTS

In His Olivet Discourse, Jesus said: "Immediately after the tribulation of those days, the sun will be darkened, and the moon will not give its light; the stars will fall from heaven, and the powers of the heavens will be shaken" (Matt 24.29).

So, not surprisingly, at the sixth Seal we read: "There was a great earthquake; and the sun became black as sackcloth of hair, and the moon became like blood. And the stars of heaven fell to the earth... then the sky receded as a scroll when it is rolled up, and every mountain and island was moved out of its place. And the kings of the earth, the great men, the rich men, the commanders, the mighty men, every slave and every free man, hid themselves in the caves and in the rocks of the mountains, and said to the mountains and rocks, 'Fall on us and hide us from the face of Him who sits on the throne and from the wrath of the Lamb! For the great day of His wrath has come, and who is able to stand?'" (Rev 6.12-17).

It is reasonable to understand "stars" as asteroids, giant meteorites and even satellites; all would appear to John as 'heavenly bodies'. This must be the same earthquake as that of Rev 16.18, which is identified as being at the time when the armies are gathered at Armageddon: "And there were noises and thunders and lightnings: and there was a great earthquake, such a mighty and great earthquake as had not occurred since men were on the earth...Then every island fled away, and the mountains were not found". This is at the juncture (Joel 3.12-16) when the nations will be assembled, the sickle will be put in, the multitudes will be gathered in the valley of decision, the sun and moon will be darkened and the Lord will roar from Zion. This will be when the Lord will show the wonders in the heaven and earth (Joel 2.30). This is what Isaiah prophesied when he wrote (and we re-quote): "The earth is violently broken, the earth is split open, and the earth is shaken exceedingly. The earth shall reel to and fro like a drunkard, and shall totter like a hut..." (Isa 24.19-21). Isaiah also goes on to talk of the assembled armies, the punishment and signs in the sun and moon.

We can scarcely take in the scale of these manifestations of God's wrath. Every city in the world will come crashing down and every mountain and island will be removed or flattened. Every ancient monument and conservation site will disappear, every bridge will collapse, every tunnel and mine will cave in. The earthquakes and tectonic movements will be on a world scale. The present configuration of the continents is largely the result of such events during the Flood. But this earthquake is said to be even greater – since men were on earth (Rev 16.18-20), in other words since before the great cordillera of the Andes was thrown up or the Mariana Trench sunk. Huge sections of seabed were lifted to the highest mountain top levels in gigantic folds. Think of the Indonesian tsunami; then think world-wide! Is there any wonder that the Bible devotes so much space to the latter days? Is it not as great a wonder that these passages are so neglected by Christians? God wants a clean sheet to start the Year of the Lord's Redeemed. Having been in Heaven with our Lord, and returning with Him as His Bride, we will see the necessity of what to us at present may seem excessive.

Those who perish at the Lord's return will, with the exception of the Beast and False Prophet, go to Sheol or Hades for the duration of the Millennium, to await the second resurrection and face Jesus Christ at the Great White Throne (Rev 20. 5 & 11-15). Only these two individuals will go directly to Gehennna; Satan will not join them for a thousand years. He is to be bound by an angel empowered so to do and will languish in the Abyss for the duration of the Year of the Lord's Redeemed. The language of Rev 20.1-3 is so clear that it is astonishing how many people, in order to support their own untenable programmes, teach that the Devil is currently bound. This will be prison security with which no earthly place of confinement can compete. Satan might outdo Houdini for his escapologist skills, but God has said that he will be bound and chained. It is a good idea to believe the Bible! In the meantime, while Satan's sentence has been pronounced, he is still free and running circles round the sceptics.

The longing of God's people down through the ages for His name to be glorified and His acts to be vindicated will now be addressed: "Will the enemy blaspheme Your name forever?...Arise, O God, plead Your own cause. Remember how the foolish man reproaches You daily...The tumult of those who rise up against You increases continually" (Ps 74.10, 22-23). God understands the frustrations of His people, but their faith and perseverance must be tested. His patience exceeds our comprehension. But He has set a time and place, and the saints of all ages will witness His victory.

The heartfelt cries of saints of many generations, who have felt the oppression of evil men, will at last be answered. Not only will wicked men receive their just rewards, so will their master. "He shall bruise your head" (Gen 3.15). Some of God's unconditional prophecies take a long time to be fulfilled, like that one; but fulfilled they most surely shall be.

CHRIST'S SECOND COMING IN POWER
Here the Day of Vengeance reaches its climax. The prophecies are numerous; we shall select a few only, and even those not necessarily in full. We have referred to others already and propose to include yet others later:-

- "O Lord God to whom vengeance belongs...shine forth! Rise up, O Judge of the earth; render punishment to the proud. Lord, how long will the wicked, how long will the wicked triumph?" (Ps 94.1-3).
- "Then the Lord (Jehovah) will go forth and fight against those nations...and in that day His feet will stand on the Mount of Olives" (Zech 14.3-4).
- "Behold, the day is coming, burning like an oven...But to you who fear My name the Sun of Righteousness shall arise with healing in His wings" (Mal 4.1-2).
- "As the lightning comes from the east and flashes to the west, so also will the coming of the Son of Man be...they will see the

Son of Man coming on the clouds of heaven with power and great glory" (Matt 24.27 & 30).

- "'This same Jesus who was taken up from you into heaven, will so come in like manner as you saw Him go into heaven.' Then they returned to Jerusalem from the mount called Olivet" (Acts 1.11-12). So called JW's hate the implications of these Zechariah and Acts verses taken together, which portray Jesus as Jehovah!

- "When the Lord Jesus is revealed from heaven with His mighty angels, in flaming fire taking vengeance on those who do not know God, and on those who do not obey the gospel of our Lord Jesus Christ" (II Thess 1.7-8).

- "Behold, the Lord comes with ten thousands of His saints, to execute judgment on all" (Jude 1.14-15).

- "Behold, He is coming with clouds, and every eye will see Him, and they also who pierced Him. And all the tribes of the earth will mourn because of Him" (Rev 1.7).

- "Then I saw heaven opened, and behold, a white horse. And He who sat on him was called Faithful and True, and in righteousness He judges and makes war...And the armies in heaven, clothed in fine linen, white and clean, followed Him on white horses. Now out of His mouth goes a sharp sword, that with it He should strike the nations. And He Himself will rule them with a rod of iron. He Himself treads the winepress of the fierceness of Almighty God. And He has on His robe and on His thigh a name written: King of Kings and Lord of Lords" (Rev 19.11,14-16).

Now the scope for study and comment is almost endless. But it is chiefly as the climax to the Day of Vengeance that we are considering these awesome prophecies. We see also hints in some of these verses of the quickly ensuing glorious Year of the Lord's Redeemed peeping over the horizon.

THE FATE OF GOD'S ENEMIES
The Revelation passage continues: "And I saw the beast, the kings of the earth and their armies, gathered together to make war against Him who sat on the horse and against His army. Then the beast was captured, and with him the false prophet who worked signs in his presence, by which he deceived those who received the mark of the beast and those who worshiped his image. These

two were cast alive into the lake of fire burning with brimstone" (Rev 19.19-20).

The Psalmist says in verses, which may have prior applications but come to full fruition here: "Why do the nations rage, and the people plot a vain thing?" (What could be more vain than this challenge?) "The kings of the earth set themselves, and the rulers take counsel together, against the Lord and against His Anointed, saying: 'Let us break their bonds in pieces and cast away their cords from us'" (this is calculated rebellion). God the Father then addresses His Son: "You shall break them with a rod of iron; You shall dash them in pieces like a potter's vessel" (Ps 2.1-3 & 9). Nahum says, "The earth heaves at His presence, yes, the world and all who dwell in it. Who can stand before His indignation? And who can endure the fierceness of His anger?" (1.5-6).

Now we cannot be specific about the timing of all deaths at this time, but it does seem that those in the armies which confront Jerusalem will be destroyed at or virtually at the moment of His Coming. "This shall be the plague with which the Lord will strike all the people who fought against Jerusalem: their flesh shall dissolve while they stand on their feet, their eyes shall dissolve in their sockets, and their tongues shall dissolve in their mouths" (Zech 14.12). "And they shall go forth and look upon the corpses of the men who have transgressed against Me" (Isa 66.24). Of the main forces at Armageddon we read: "And the rest were killed with the sword which proceeded from the mouth of Him who sat on the horse" (Rev 19.21).

As for those who are not on the immediate field of battle at this time, we read: "They shall go into the holes of the rocks, and into the caves of the earth, from the terror of the Lord and the glory of His majesty, when He arises to shake the earth mightily" (Isa 2.19). This confirms that the sixth Seal, which described the same event, occurs at the end of the Great Tribulation (Rev 6.15-16). We will return to these events later.

Within these first days the Lord evidently has other 'military' matters to deal with. Isaiah asks: "'Who is this who comes from Edom, with dyed garment from Bozrah?...Why is Your apparel red and Your garments like one who treads in the winepress?' 'I have trodden the winepress alone, and from the peoples no one was with Me, for I have trodden them in My anger, and trampled them in My fury...for **the Day of Vengeance is in My heart**, and the Year of My Redeemed has come'" (Isa 63.1-4). This would suggest that dealing with Edom, a neighbouring Semitic age-old oppressor of Israel, is not the Lord's first priority, although there is a minority view that Jesus will return to Edom before Jerusalem. "Remember O Lord, against the sons of Edom the day of Jerusalem, who said 'Raze it, raze it to its very foundation!'" (Ps 137.7). It may very well be that this may be to do with the recovery of those faithful Jews who have been provided with a desert refuge for three and a half years. They have to be brought home.

JUDGMENTS AT THE SECOND COMING

Jesus said that He did not come to judge the world at His First Coming, but that He would do so at His Second Coming, eg Matt 25.31 et seq. There are in fact to be several different judgments at this time. Some obviously come either earlier or later than others, but putting all into a definite sequence is impossible for us at present. Where sentencing is involved, some will be instantaneous; others will involve confinement to await a further judgment later.

Punitive judgments:
- Judgment of Satan
- Judgment of Antichrist and the False Prophet
- Judgment of the armies at Armageddon and Jerusalem

Judgment of life and service for reward and recognition:
- Judgment of the resurrected Old Testament saints
- Judgment of the Tribulation martyrs

Judgment to decide destinies for the Millennium:
- Judgment of the Nations – the surviving Gentiles ("sheep and goats")
- Judgment of the surviving Jews ("one third and two thirds")

How strange it is that the idea of a single general judgment, with its roots in paganism, should prevail even within Christian churches, simply because the Bible does not always specify a particular judgment. No believer will be judged for sins, which were paid for by Christ's vicarious death on Calvary, but every raptured believer will, whilst in Heaven, have had his or her service for the Lord judged at the Bema or Judgment Seat of Christ (I Cor 3.13-16, II Cor 5.10). The bema was the place where laurel wreaths and other tributes were given to competitors in ancient games. This must be before the Marriage of the Lamb (Rev 19.7), and will probably be immediately after the Rapture. We recall that time scales do not count in Heaven; all will be thorough and scrupulously fair. As we shall see in our next chapter, the judgment of the unsaved will take place after the end of the world (Rev 20.11).

We will deal in this chapter with the immediate punitive judgments and with those which will decide the destiny of survivors of the Great Tribulation.

THE JUDGMENT OF THE NATIONS_

In Joel 3.11-12 we read God's command: "Assemble and come, all you nations, and gather together all around...Let the nations be wakened, and come up to the Valley of Jehoshaphat; for there I will sit to judge all the surrounding nations". The following verse places the event as to timing by referring to the same astronomical and atmospheric phenomena as other Tribulation passages. So this is one of the events connected to the Lord's return. Moreover it deals with Gentiles, not Jews. This is not Armageddon, where death will be without trial, the participation in the blasphemous armies being cause enough.

This judgment will be centred at Jerusalem. The Valley of Jehoshaphat, according to Unger's Bible Dictionary, is the Kidron Valley, between Jerusalem and the Mount of Olives. Although we can find plenty of instances in Scripture where God either blesses or judges specific nations for their behaviour or sin, this is not about judging nations as such, but about judging every Gentile or individual from the nations. It deals with the same matters as Jesus foretold in Matt 25.31-46.

Chapter headings in the Bible are neither inspired nor infallible.

They can be helpful, but also confusing. For nearly four hundred years most editions of the AV have given this Matthew passage the misleading title, 'a description of the last judgment'. The NLB's 'the final judgment' is equally dangerous. The NIV uses the title 'the sheep and the goats', which is reasonable; the NASB uses the non-committal, 'the judgment'; JND, the Amplified and RSV all play safe with no titles. NKJV gives 'the Judgment of the Nations'. Several other variations exist. However we are happy with the NKJV description, which is fully consistent with the text of this passage.

This is no trivial matter of prejudice for or against certain versions. There is a fundamental theological doctrine at stake here. If this is indeed the *last* judgement, then Paul and five centuries of Protestants are wrong – salvation is of works!!! Now to us, that, as Paul says in Gal 1.6-9, is anathema – another Gospel. Let us look briefly at the passage, which is a continuation of Jesus' Olivet Discourse and which follows on from two parables. It is emphatically not a parable, although Jesus does use the simile – "He will separate them one from another, **as** a shepherd divides his sheep from the goats" (v.32).

"When the Son of Man comes in His glory, and all the holy angels with Him, then He will sit on the throne of His glory, and all the nations will be gathered before Him." (v.31). This is unquestionably one of the events which will immediately follow His return in glory as described in Rev 19. So it is upon earth, with a location specified, and therefore in stark contrast to the Great White Throne, more than a thousand years later when this world has passed away (Rev 20.11). So the Judgment of the Nations cannot be the last judgment. The later Great White Throne uses the main criterion of whether names are written in the Lamb's Book of life (Rev 20.15). In the Judgment of the Nations the criterion is the treatment of "these, My brethren" (v.40). This passage is unique in that, if one ignores the context, one might get the impression that salvation is through charitable works – through visiting the sick, the suffering, the imprisoned. There appears to be no mention of salvation through faith, or of redemption through Christ's blood.

In no way are we demeaning the importance of charitable works.

Believers in the Church Age may one day be commended for them, but never saved by them. We must remember that those who will appear at this judgment will have lived through the Great Tribulation, when people will either have sold themselves to the Devil through the Mark of the Beast and be beyond repentance, or will have courageously resisted and taken a stand on the Lord's side. Charitable works, which are at present not uncommon among unbelievers as well as believers, will doubtless at that time be absent in the unbelieving, as the result of the hardening of hearts involved in accepting the Mark. The cost of daring to help "these My brethren", whom in our fourth chapter we identified as Jewish evangelists, will be incalculable. Those who support them will be nailing their colours to the mast and identifying with these evangelists and their message.

The Gospel of the Kingdom is to be preached in all the world, "and then the end will come" (Matt 24.14); every single person standing before the Son of Man will have experienced some sort of meaningful witness or call to repentance as a result of this special ministry. It is not unreasonable to believe that the evangelists will have a truly Pentecostal gift of tongues, a miraculously imparted facility to enable everyone to hear the Gospel in his own language,

Paul Benware writes: "Those who are the righteous among the Gentiles (the "sheep") will be welcomed into Messiah's kingdom, but those who are unsaved (the "goats") will be sent away into everlasting punishment. The internal, spiritual condition of the Gentiles is revealed externally by the way in which they treated Israel during the Great Tribulation. This is valid proof of true righteousness because of the terrible persecution that Israel will endure during the second half of the Tribulation. For a Gentile to treat any Jewish person with kindness during the Tribulation will put his life in jeopardy. No one will do this merely out of beneficent attitude, but only out of a redeemed heart." (Understanding End Times Prophecy).

The only reservation one might make about the above quotation is that it will almost certainly be the treatment of the Jewish evangelists who preach repentance – modern John the Baptists

– who will go into all countries, rather than the treatment of all Israel, which will be the deciding factor. Israel will still include apostate Jews who will initially welcome the Antichrist as their saviour. This of course in no way whatsoever excuses the persecution of such apostate Jews. God will hold no persecutor of any Jew guiltless.

We cannot give an exact timescale for this judgment. But there is a statement which has attracted much speculation in Dan 12.12, "Blessed is he who waits, and comes to the one thousand three hundred and thirty-five days". The days are measured from the Abomination, so an extension of seventy five days beyond the 1,260 days (Rev 11.3) is indicated. Those who survive are to be blessed. We cannot be adamant, but it does appear that the swift retributive judgment of Armageddon and the judicial assizes of the Valley of Jehoshaphat, the binding of Satan and other events to wind up the Day of Vengeance will extend for seventy-five days, only then will the Year of the Lord's Redeemed commence.

How Christ will judge so many in so short a time is a question which need not concern us. He is Almighty God; nobody, be they 'sheep' or 'goat' will be unfairly judged. Even though the world population will have been reduced by billions during the Great Tribulation and the following earthquake, and despite the destruction of the colossal armies, there will still be hundreds of millions to be brought to Jerusalem for trial. Roads and railways will have been destroyed and airlines grounded. But the God who will have previously caused the entire living Church plus the even greater numbers of believing dead, to be caught up into Heaven, will be able to perform this miracle too. We will see more of these "sheep" and their glorious future in our final chapter. God's vengeance will fall on the "goats".

VENGEANCE ON SELECTED JEWS
"And it shall come to pass in all the land, says the Lord, that two thirds in it shall be cut off and die, but one third shall be left in it: I will bring the one third through the fire, will refine them as silver is refined, and test them as gold is tested. They will call on My name, and I will answer them. I will say, 'This is My people'; and each one will say, 'The Lord is my God'" (Zech 13.8-9).

In our fifth chapter we noted that God's 'wrath' rather than His 'vengeance' is normally applied to Jews, and all the instances of divine vengeance that we have looked at hitherto have involved the nations or Gentiles. However God's ancient people are not exempt when terminal apostasy is involved – apostasy taking the soul beyond the point of no return. It is primarily regarding Israel that God first said: "Vengeance is Mine, and recompense...for the Lord will judge His people" (Deut 32.35-36). Apostate Jews have long felt God's vengeance, and this will continue until practically the end of the Great Tribulation. God says to them: "I will make you pass under the rod, I will bring you into the bond of the covenant; I will purge the rebels from among you" (Ezek 20.37-38). This process has been going on through all the centuries of the *Diaspora*, but for some it will culminate within the Land.

Whether the two thirds will simply perish, to await the later Great White Throne or will first face Christ at a separate tribunal, as each surviving Gentile will, is not absolutely clear. But it does seem from the Zechariah 13 passage quoted above that the final holocaust days of the Great Tribulation will constitute the judgment, and that the outcome will be, for those being saved as they repent and recognise their Messiah-Saviour, entry into the Millennial kingdom. They will be included in 'My Redeemed'. Those who earlier had exercised faith by heeding Jesus' injunction to flee when the Abomination of Desolation was set up will, we assume have been saved already.

Baron says: "If we interpret Scripture rightly, they (Jews who are in Jerusalem at that time) shall have entered into covenant and sworn allegiance to a false Messiah, thus culminating their national apostasy, and fulfilling the word of Christ, 'If another shall come in his own name, him ye shall receive'." (The Visions & Prophecies of Zechariah). We have already noted that, if this relationship has been sealed by acceptance of the Mark of the Beast, there can be no salvation (Rev 14.11). As far as the Jews are concerned, the acceptance or rejection of the Mark could be the deciding factor as to whether people will be in the two thirds or one third...Certainly no devout Jew could lightly accept such a mark, without recognising its idolatrous implications.

As we have noted, for a brief period the situation in the city will be dire. For a moment, it seems, the Lord's defence of the city, referred to above, will be relaxed, though no doubt here also the third who are to survive will have a degree of special protection. "The Lord will judge His people and have compassion on His servants, when He sees that their power is gone" (Deut 32.36). Never in all the centuries of self inflicted Anti-Semitism will their plight be quite as desperate. Never will grief and repentance for spiritual blindness and stubbornness be so keenly felt as when "they will mourn for Him as one mourns for his only son" (Zech 12.10). Their Saviour and Deliverer will be Jehovah who goes forth to fight for them, Jehovah, whose once pierced feet will stand upon the Mount of Olives, which will thereupon split asunder. The despised and rejected Jesus Christ will be seen by Israel as being the honoured and revered Jehovah. Zechariah 14.3-4 is quite clear about this.

THE DARKEST HOUR BEFORE THE DAWN
Let us close by following Dr Fred Tatford's example in 'The Climax Of The Ages', and quoting from the eloquent pen of Joseph Seiss in his masterly 1865 four volume commentary on Revelation. "The sun frowns, the day is neither light nor dark. The mountains melt and cleave asunder at His presence. The hills bound from their seats and skip like lambs. The sea rolls back with howling trepidation. The sky is rent and folds upon itself like a collapsed tent. It is the day for executing an armed world – a world in covenant with hell to overthrow the authority and throne of God – and everything is terrified. Nature joins to signalize the deserved vengeance. So the Scriptures everywhere represent."

The blasphemously ignorant have commented that, were Jesus to return today, He would have to adjust His ideas. Such is the arrogance of mankind and the distortion of what is pure and what is perverted, that the 'Bible' of the politically correct assumes more authority than the Holy Word of God. "You, Lord, in the beginning laid the foundation of the earth, and the heavens are the works of Your hands. They will perish, but You remain; and they will all grow old like a garment; like a cloak You will fold them up, and they will be changed. But You are the same, and Your years will not fail" (Heb 1.10-12).

Certain versions of the Bible have recently been edited to make them politically and culturally correct. Unless they repent and reverse their deeds, God will not hold the perpetrators guiltless. To tamper with the prophetic word is an invitation to vengeance. If anyone adds to these things, God will add to him the plagues that are written in this book; and if anyone takes away from the words of the book of this prophecy, God shall take away his part from the Book of Life, from the holy city and from the things which are written in this book (Rev 22.18-19). Pastors, ministers and leaders of congregations or assemblies have no need to be preoccupied by prophecy; but those who, either out of apathy or fear of being unpopular, omit to preach and teach what God has so graciously revealed about the latter days, take upon themselves a grave responsibility. Even producing politically correct hymnbooks is an exceedingly dangerous ploy.

He who made the worlds out of nothing alone sets a true plumb-line, righteous scales, true standards. And man has not only fallen woefully short, but in recent decades, in the public media and in law courts, he has openly defied what previously had at least been acknowledged, even if rarely kept. That overweening arrogance which will make the Beast, the kings of the earth and their armies think that they can fight against "Him that sat on the horse and against His army" (Rev 19:19) is already much in evidence. "Thrust in your sickle and reap, for the time has come for You to reap, for the harvest of the earth is ripe" (Rev 14.15).

For the persistently rebellious, the Coming in Power portends the greatest imaginable terror and the most appalling of fates. "For behold, the day is coming, burning like an oven, and all the proud, yes, all who do wickedly will be stubble, and the day which is coming shall burn them up' says the Lord of Hosts...'But to you who fear My name, the Sun of Righteousness shall arise with healing in His wings'" (Mal 4.1-2).

Thus we come to the end of our review of the Day of Vengeance of our God. It would be appropriate to close with words of a great Psalm, which has sometimes been misapplied to Jesus' ascension, but in fact refers to His return to Jerusalem at His Second Coming. "Lift up your heads, O you gates! And be lifted up, you everlasting doors! And the King of glory shall come in. Who is this King of glory? The

Lord, strong and mighty, the Lord mighty in battle" (Ps 24.7-8). We re-quote Matt 23.37-39: "O Jerusalem, Jerusalem...you shall see Me no more till you say. 'Blessed is He who comes in the name of the Lord'". At His Return in Power this condition will at last be met. The Year of the Lord's Redeemed will be about to commence.

God's first course was to send His only Begotten Son to the world which He loved. Vengeance follows only long term rejection of that offer. As Christians we should love the world. Any religion where fervour is measured by the level of our murderous activities against others can only be of the Devil, "who was a murderer from the beginning" (Jn 8.44).

CHAPTER SEVEN

The Year of My Redeemed

SCENES HARD TO VISUALISE

"The day of vengeance is in My heart, and the year of My redeemed has come". As we read again that prophetic utterance of the Messiah in Isaiah 63, it seems that the words are spoken in a single breath; the two thoughts are inseparable. The second is impossible without the first. One is stupendously solemn, the other is wondrously joyful. We are reminded of those lovely words of the Psalmist, "Weeping may endure for a night, but joy comes in the morning" (30.5). We have allowed ourselves only one chapter to cover the Year of My Redeemed, as we did with the Acceptable Year. It is an awesome task

The number of texts we can choose from is legion; the Psalms and prophetic books are full of references to Israel's and the world's ultimate golden era. But, as with the Great Tribulation, we shall be relying on the grand old book of Revelation to put things into perspective. Elsewhere we are bombarded with exciting information, but in Revelation 19 and 20 we find a sequence which brings the other events into a coherent, comprehensible programme.

This side of the Rapture we are in mortal bodies, with mortal mind-sets, and will therefore find it much easier to comprehend or visualise those prophecies which refer to mortals in the restored creation. It is more difficult to visualise roles and activities of immortals – ourselves and other resurrected saints in their resurrection bodies.

While it may seem easy to picture our Lord as His feet touch down on the Mount of Olives, or as He sits on His throne to judge the Sheep and the Goats, we must remember who He is. He is the eternal Son of God, who, at a point in time, also became the Son of Man. God the Father "has spoken to us by His Son, whom He has appointed heir of all things, through whom also He made the worlds; who being the brightness of His glory and the express image of His person, and upholding all things by the word of His power, when He had by Himself purged our sins, sat down at the right hand of the Majesty on high" (Heb1.2-3). Thus the One who will rule from Zion is also the One who controls the most far-flung galaxies.

It is easy to have a naïve and parochial view of our returning Saviour. We have no way this side of glory of comprehending these matters, and should never be ashamed to admit it. But the fact that He has purged our sins as well as fulfilling all these august roles gives us supreme confidence. If we must wonder, let it be about His immeasurable love that once compelled Him to lay aside that glory, which once more He owns in Heaven (Jn 17.5) and is yet to receive on earth. We can learn a valuable lesson from the experience of the venerable apostle John. Nobody was closer to Him during His earthly ministry; yet he records that, when he saw Him in His resurrection body, he fell at His feet as one dead (Rev 1.17).

THE MILLENNIUM
We have already seen clear-cut statements about a thousand years, the collective word for which is 'Millennium'. Early in our book we observed that when Scripture gives a specific figure, it means precisely what it says. So let us summarise briefly in the sequence given in Revelation 20 what is said there to last a thousand years.

- Satan will be confined in the bottomless pit for a thousand years (v.2).
- Satan will not deceive the nations for a thousand years (v.3).
- Resurrected martyrs will live and reign with Christ for a thousand years (v.4).
- Thus Christ Himself will reign for a thousand years (v.4).
- The rest of the dead will remain dead for a thousand years (v.5).
- All resurrected saints will reign with Christ for a thousand years (v.6).

At the end of the thousand years Satan will be released for a short period (v.7).

In view of the above, what folly it is to teach, as some do, that the present Church Age is the Millennium! If Satan is not deceiving the nations now, whoever is? The Church Age has been the greater part of the Acceptable Year of the Lord. Now we come to the Year of the Lord's Redeemed. It is one thing to quibble with the meaning of a vision, but when the vision of Satan's binding in verse 1 is plainly interpreted for our comprehension, as is in vv.2 and 7, it is an affront to the sanctity of the Bible to do anything other than to take it at face value.

Let us make some general observations about the Millennium. We will be returning to most of these later, when we will give references.

• Like the Acceptable Year of the Lord, it is to be a long period of time, in contrast with the much shorter Day of Vengeance of our God.

• The repeated emphasis given to a thousand years in Revelation 20 gives us every reason to believe that it will last precisely that number of years.

• The Millennium will take place upon earth. It is not in Heaven.

• The resurrected or raptured saints of the Old Testament, the Church Age and the Tribulation will all be present, but in their celestial bodies.

• When the kingdoms of this world have been wrenched from the Beast, the kingdom and dominion shall be given to the saints of the Most High (Dan 7.27).

• The "blessed of the Lord", whom we have seen as the 'sheep' of Matthew 25, will be saved before entering the Millennium.

• These survivors of the Great Tribulation and their descendants will populate the earth.

- Although Satan will be bound throughout the Millennium, the total absence of sin, as foretold for the New Heaven and Earth (Rev 21 & 22), will not yet apply.

- There will be an entirely new covenant; but those born during the Millennium will be required to be saved just as we are. Individual salvation will be no less necessary than now.

- The curse imposed at the Fall of Man in Eden will be lifted from the earth and from nature; this will be the 'Utopia' which men through the ages have longed for. But it will be so only on God's terms.

- Jesus Christ will reign over the entire world from Jerusalem with a rod of iron. God's special covenant with David will be honoured, and he will rule as prince of Israel under the High King, as it were.

- The twelve apostles will sit on thrones to judge the twelve tribes.

- "The earth will be filled with the knowledge of the glory of the Lord, as the waters cover the sea" (Is 11.9 & Hab 2.14).

- This reign will be marked by peace, prosperity and righteousness.

- The resurrection of the 'dry bones' of Ezekiel 37 will be fully accomplished at the outset.

- The Chosen People will at long last be internationally respected – "the head and not the tail" (Deut 28.13).

- Judah and Israel will at last be re-united, and Israel will no longer be in rebellion against the house of David.

- There will be a magnificent temple in Jerusalem (Ezek 40-46). In it, but apparently nowhere else, there will be memorial, rather than efficacious, animal sacrifices.

CHRIST'S RIGHTEOUS REIGN

In the same hymnbook we may encounter the lines: "Jesus shall reign where'er the sun, doth his successive journeys run", and also "He is crowned, King of the whole world crowned, ruling the nations now." Both cannot be right. Zechariah 14 confirms that it is the older, the first hymn, which is correct. Many modern song writers seem to be producing, no doubt with the best of intentions and with the idea of bringing glory to their Lord, songs which are only cursorily checked with Scripture. It is no trivial matter, because outsiders hear these words and see little evidence of Jesus' righteous reign in the world, and assume that it is the Bible rather than the lyric writer that is wrong. The hymn, "I cannot tell..." is another which gets it right, describing the future circumstances and concluding with: "At last the Saviour, Saviour of the world, is King."

It is when Jesus' feet stand on the Mount of Olives that "the Lord shall be King over all the earth" (Zech 14.3 & 9). It is when He descends from Heaven with a sharp two edged sword to strike the nations that "He Himself will rule them with a rod of iron" (Rev 19.15). In the meantime, while it is perfectly true that "the Most High rules in the kingdom of men (Dan 4.17), He is neither recognised nor crowned by the vast bulk of this world's population or its rulers. That time is still ahead.

"'Behold, the days are coming' says the Lord, 'that I will raise to David a Branch of righteousness; a King shall reign and prosper, and execute judgment and righteousness in the earth. In His days Judah will be saved and dwell safely; now this is His name by which He will be called; THE LORD OUR RIGHTEOUSNESS'" (Jer 23.5-6). "You shall call His name Jesus. He will be great, and will be called the Son of the Highest; and the Lord will give Him the throne of His Father David. And He will reign over the house of Jacob for ever, and of His kingdom there will be no end (Lk 1.31-33). "And His name will be called Wonderful, Counsellor, Mighty God, Everlasting Father, Prince of Peace. Of the increase of His government and peace there will be no end, upon the throne of David and over his kingdom, to order it and establish it with judgment and justice from that time forward, even for ever" (Isa 9.6-7). These familiar passages are primarily Messianic, with the most explicit and unambiguous references to Israel. Similar prophecies refer to His reign from Zion.

Later the angel of the Lord announced that the good tidings were for all people (Lk 2.10); there are two parallel sets of truths here. By no stretch of the imagination can they be said to have been fulfilled; and we are certainly not about to suggest that God's promise to Mary through Gabriel was unfaithful. Eventually the kingdom will be transferred to the new creation, but it must first exist on earth during the Millennium in the precise terms of these prophecies.

Those who indulge in the seventeen hundred year old practice of denying the future literal Millennial reign of Christ take upon themselves a huge responsibility. Dr Dwight Pentecost writes: "Establishing the rule of David's Son as Sovereign over the earth demonstrates that Satan's kingdom is a false kingdom. Apart from the reign of Christ in a Davidic kingdom here on earth, God's promises and God's covenants would have failed. And apart from this rule, God's purposes for man would never be brought to a conclusion. God's purposes for earth would be unrealised and the problem generated by Satan's rebellion would never be resolved. Thus the physical, literal reign of Christ on earth is a theological and biblical necessity – unless Satan is victorious over God" (Thy Kingdom Come).

WHO ARE THESE REDEEMED?
There will be five classes of redeemed during the Millennium. There will be:

- Those in immortal bodies - Old Testament saints, Church and Tribulation martyrs.
- Jews who will have heeded the warning to escape, and who were in a place of refuge during the Great Tribulation.
- Jews who will repent when they recognise their Messiah, whether they were in the Land or elsewhere.
- The Gentile 'sheep' who will have been saved before the end of the Great Tribulation.
- Those born during the Millennium who have a saving faith.

When we talk about the redeemed in a general context, we might be referring to any blood- bought group of believers of any race or dispensation. There never has been and never will be any other form of salvation. We could argue convincingly from Scripture that, had any other means of salvation been available, God would not have given His Only Begotten Son. There is no doubt that all redeemed of all the ages will be participants in and beneficiaries of the Millennial Kingdom in one way or another. Those in mortal bodies and those in resurrection bodies will have different responsibilities and different needs.

However, if we look at Isa 63.4, quoted at the very beginning of our book and at the start of this chapter, whether within its surrounding verses or within the latter twenty-seven chapters of Isaiah, it is obvious that the redeemed, when they are referred to thus, constitute a very specific group. The Jamieson-Fausset-Brown Commentary renders 'My redeemed' as 'My people *to be redeemed*', implying the then living, rather than the previously dead. Both the narrower and the wider contexts are about Israel. This does not mean that there are no spiritual lessons or applications for the Church. But it is not primarily *about* the Church. The Year of My Redeemed therefore applies primarily to mortal saints of Israel, even if the rest of us have a share. The Church's inheritance is in Heaven.

Before we look at the resurrected or translated redeemed, we will consider those who will be alive on earth in their mortal bodies during the Millennium, and see what kind of restored planet they will live in.

THE REDEEMED OF ISRAEL
Three of the four references to 'the redeemed' (Hebrew *gaal*), in the major and minor prophets apply quite unambiguously to Israel; only the Isa 35.9 reference could possibly be interpreted more widely. In the same section of Scripture almost all of the thirteen instances of the active verb 'redeemed' apply similarly, including specific references to Abraham and to Jacob (Isa 29.22, 43.1, 44.23, 48.20, Jer 31.11). In Mic 6.4 God says: "I redeemed you from the house of bondage; and I sent before you Moses and Aaron and Miriam". This is Israel.

"The ransomed of the Lord shall return, and come to Zion with singing, with everlasting joy on their heads. They shall obtain joy and gladness, and sorrow and sighing shall flee away" (Isa 35.10 & 51.11). It has recently been set to music, and is sometimes sung as if it applied primarily to the Church, which is silly and sad. This is the future Year of My Redeemed. It is not talking about the Jews who are currently still returning piecemeal to Israel at present. They may sing, but, unless they accept Christ as their Saviour first, they will have to endure the world's worst holocaust before there is any prospect of everlasting joy upon their heads. That does not mean that we should discourage them, or that there is no joy to be had in returning. It is after all their land. We simply must not give them premature expectations, by concealing their immediate individual need for Christ as Saviour-Messiah. Their future completed return, when God sets up His banner, is to be world-wide (Isa 11.11-12).

Repentance must come first: "'In those days and at that time' says the Lord, 'the children of Israel shall come, they and the children of Judah together; with continual weeping they shall come, and seek the Lord their God. They shall ask the way to Zion, with their faces toward it, saying, "Come and let us join ourselves to the Lord in a perpetual covenant that will not be forgotten" (Jer 50.4-5). There are still more Jews scattered around the world than there are in Israel. Their future departure from their lands of exile seems to be despondent, but their arrival in their own Land is to be joyful. It seems that they will have been convicted during the Great Tribulation but understandably unable to travel. We saw in our previous chapter something of the repentance of the inhabitants of Jerusalem.

Repentance is always a prerequisite for redemption, so it is appropriate that we should then find: "In that day a fountain shall be opened for the house of David and for the inhabitants of Jerusalem, for sin and uncleanness" (Zech 13.1). There is much, much more revealed about the penitence and restitution of Israel. "In the place where it was said to them, 'You are not My people,' there it shall be said to them, you are the sons of the living God" (Hos 1.10). "'This is the covenant I will make with the house of Israel after those days', says the Lord: 'I will put My law in their minds, and write it on their hearts; and I will be their God, and they shall be My people. No more shall every man teach his neighbour, and every man his brother, saying, "Know the Lord," for they shall all know Me from the least of them to the greatest of them, says the Lord'"(Jer 31.33-34).

There have indeed been partial fulfilments of these two passages in the return from the Babylonian exile, but nothing on the scale or in the detail which would signal a complete fulfilment. Neither has anything along these lines happened in the Church Age.

The Gentile 'sheep' will also have been wonderfully redeemed, but the promise is firstly and primarily to Israel. Much in recent years has been made of Ezekiel 37 and the vision of the Dry Bones regarding the recent history of the nation, Israel. But this is only partial and preparatory. William Kelly calls it "A striking vision with a plain explanation. It is a question neither of the conversion of the soul **nor of the resurrection of the body,** but of God's causing Israel to live once more by-and-by as a nation." Later he adds: "These bones are the whole house of Israel'...He (God) declares that He will not only disinter them from the graves where they now lie buried as a nation, but He will bring them into the land of Israel – an issue suitable not to those risen from the dead". (Notes on Ezekiel).

Kelly was writing nearly a century ago, and while, like other Pre-Millennialists, he had faith to believe implicitly in the rebirth of Israel, he did not anticipate the long delay between the rebirth of the nation and the ultimate revival. But in the eyes of the world Israel is again a nation, whether its right to exist is recognised or not. Politically, militarily and economically Israel may be alive, but spiritually she is still dead, blind to the identity of her Messiah, unrepentant as to His crucifixion. God has yet to put His spirit into the dead bones. The fact that very few Jews can trace their tribal descent, since records were burnt in the Temple in 70 AD, does not mean that the 'united stick' in God's hand has now materialised in some vague symbolic way (Ezek 37.15-22). God's promise is explicit. We have seen from Revelation 7 that God knows the tribal pedigree of each individual. When Christ returns and that knowledge is disclosed, the three thousand year old rift which occurred in the generation after Solomon (I Kings 12.17-19) will be publicly healed and divinely sanctioned and supervised (v.22). Israel will at last fulfil its function of being a light to the Gentiles (Isa 42.6, 60.3), and be a kingdom of priests (Ex 19.6), intermediaries between the Gentiles and God.

Those Christians who cry 'not fair' to God's special treatment of Israel forget five things:-

- He is God, with absolute rights. "Woe to him who strives with his Maker!...Shall the clay say to him who forms it, 'What are you making?'" (Isa 45.9).
- Jesus was a Jew!
- Israel's special privileges down through the ages have always been balanced by Israel's special responsibilities. It is idle to envy one and not the other.
- As illustrated in the parable of the workers in the vineyard (Matt 20.1-15), God does not deprive one by being generous to another. "Is your eye evil because I am good?" (v.15). In fact down through the ages Israel, admittedly because of her own sin, has probably suffered more than she has been blessed. At long last that will change.
- Being a member of the Church of Jesus Christ is greater honour than being a Jew.

The disillusioned pair walking to Emmaus told Jesus, the risen Jesus whom they had not recognised, "We were hoping that it was He who was going to redeem Israel" (Lk 24.21). There is no hint that these prophecies became null and void when the Church was born. Gabriel's promise to Mary has never been revoked: "He will be great and will be called the Son of the Highest; and the Lord God will give Him the throne of His father David" (Lk 1.32).

"'Comfort, yes, comfort My people!' says your God. 'Speak comfort to Jerusalem and cry out to her that her warfare is ended, that her iniquity is pardoned; for she has received from the Lord's hand double for her sins.'...The glory of the Lord shall be revealed, and all flesh shall see it together; for the mouth of the Lord has spoken...Say to the cities of Judah, 'Behold your God!' Behold, the Lord God shall come..." (Isa 40.1 *et seq*).

Jerusalem is also said to be redeemed: "The LORD has comforted His people, He has redeemed Jerusalem" (Isa 52.9) and "You shall be called 'Sought Out', a city not forsaken" (Isa 62.12). It is to Jerusalem that the Conquering Messiah will return. We know that "His feet will stand on the Mount of Olives which faces Jerusalem on the east". (Zech 14.4). We know that He will first approach the city from the east (Ezek 44.1, 2), just as it was from the east that the glory of the Lord departed in Ezekiel's own time (11.23). We know that it is from Jerusalem that He will reign throughout the Millennium, though from the last nine chapters of Ezekiel we know that it is going to be a very different and very wonderful Jerusalem.

Jesus told His disciples that they would sit on twelve thrones judging the tribes of Israel (Lk 22.30). This does not necessarily imply a single judgment, such as that described at the resurrection of the Tribulation martyrs; it is more likely that they will throughout the Millennium fulfil roles such as that described in Ex 18.22, when Moses delegated to tribal leaders power to deal with all but the most serious cases. Unlike those men of old, they, being immortal, will be completely fair, incorruptible and unable to be deceived. Ezekiel chapter 48 gives an entirely new tribal allocation to Israel; that which took place in Joshua's day was imperfect, some of the tribes having pre-empted the decision making.

In that Great Tribulation passage in Daniel 12 we read: "Those who are wise shall shine like the brightness of the firmament, and those who turn many to righteousness like the stars for ever" (v.3). Surely few will qualify for this description more than the 144,000 Jewish evangelists, whom we have already seen described as "these My brethren". God will give places of honour to those who have truly earned them, and for them we suspect that this will be within the Israel from which they were first sent out.

THE REDEEMED OF THE GENTILES

In Isaiah 2 and a parallel passage in Micah 4 we find: "Now it shall come to pass in the latter days that the mountain of the Lord's house shall be established on the top of the mountains, and shall be exalted above the hills; and peoples shall flow to it. Many nations shall come and say, 'Come, and let us go up to the mountain of the Lord, to the house of the God of Jacob and He will teach us His ways, and we shall walk in His paths'" (Isa 2.2-3 & Mic 4.1-2). "'The glory of this latter temple shall be greater than the former' says the Lord of Hosts. 'And in this place I will give peace'" (Hag 2.9). Haggai gives the setting – it follows God's shaking of heaven, earth, sea and dry land. None of this has happened yet.

At the Judgment of the Nations Jesus will say to the 'sheep': "Come, you blessed of My Father, inherit the kingdom prepared for you from the foundation of the world" (Matt 25.34). The Millennial kingdom is no afterthought; rather it is a state that has been in suspension since the Fall of man in Eden. In Isa 65.23 we read of those born in the Millennium: "They shall be the descendants of the blessed of the Lord, and their offspring with them". Unlike the resurrected saints who do not marry (Matt 22.30), these people will rear families as we do now. In view of this, how strange it is that people confuse the Judgment of the Nations with the last judgment.

According to Isaiah 65, people will live as long as trees (v.22). Methuselah's record will at last be broken, as the 'sheep', who entered the Millennial kingdom on day one survive unto the very end; at least we have no evidence to the contrary, although they will eventually grow old. But children will be born to them (v.23). "Old men and old women shall again sit in the streets of Jerusalem, each one with his staff in his hand because of great age. The streets of the city shall be full of boys and girls playing in its streets" (Zech 8.4-5).

Unlike the New Heaven and Earth, death will not be unknown, but the human lifespan will be comparable to or greater than before the Flood. "No more shall an infant from there live but a few days, nor an old man who has not fulfilled his days; but the child shall die one hundred years old, but the sinner being one hundred years old shall be accursed...As the days of a tree, so shall be the days of My people" (Isa 65.20, 22).

Sin will not be totally eliminated. There will be no external tempter, but, despite the perfect living conditions, people will be able to harbour rebellion in their hearts. Worship will be obligatory and should be a welcome and natural activity; man's first duty is to worship His Creator. But penalties have already been stipulated for those individuals or communities who fail to come to the annual Feast of Tabernacles (Zech 14.17-19). Sin will be punishable by instant death (Isa 11.4, 65.20).

This is why memorial blood sacrifices will be performed in the Millennial Temple. There are several references to such sacrifices, but Ezek 43.19-27 is the only passage giving details. Just as they offered Levitical sacrifices, which God well knew would never be efficacious for cleansing from sin, yet were ordained by Him to look forward to Calvary, so memorial sacrifices, looking back to Calvary, will be made for those still in their mortal bodies and requiring salvation. This is not a popular teaching, but it is clearly enough stated and easy to understand. God has ordained it, and the misapplication of certain verses in the book of Hebrews will not disprove it.

Here are reminders that the Millennium is not to be confused with the eternal state, where nothing which defiles will be permitted to exist (Rev 22.15). Nevertheless Satan will be locked away, enlightenment will abound, all religion will be pure, conditions will be perfect. However not all sin stems from the tempter. The teaching of behavioural psychologists that sin is the result of environment is a fallacy; at best the environment may exacerbate the inherent waywardness of man that dates back to the Fall. Everyone born during the Millennium will have to be saved – truly born again. But some may profess salvation but retain rebellious hearts. This explains the several references to Jesus ruling with a rod of iron.

The Gentiles will benefit as much as the Jews from all the material and most of the spiritual blessings enumerated above. What about the other differences? As we have already observed, the greatest privileges and the correspondingly greatest responsibilities are accorded to the Jews. But the ancient promise to Abraham will still hold good, "In you all the families of the earth shall be blessed" (Gen 12.3). This applies of course to the gift to the world of the Saviour, the greatest blessing of all, but it has many wider implications too. "The nations shall bless themselves in Him, and in Him they shall glory" (Jer 4.2). In Isa19.23 we read that the Egyptians and Assyrians will come to worship and share a blessing with Israel. Well, that has certainly never happened before! "His name shall endure for ever; His name shall continue as long as the sun, and men shall be blessed in Him; and all nations shall call Him blessed." (Ps 72.17).

Isaiah 65 tells us a good deal more about life and conditions in the Millennium. Unlike Revelation 20 and 21, it does not differentiate between the Millennium and the eternal state.

A RESTORED ENVIRONMENT
God gave man dominion over the works of His hands (Gen 1.28, Ps 8.6). But we have abused that responsibility; before the Lord returns pollution may be expected to be beyond control. The environmental devastation of the world through judgment will also be well nigh total by the end of the Great Tribulation. Two of the final calamities will be the rolling up of the atmosphere – "The sky receded as a scroll" (Isa 34.4 & Rev 6.14) and the world-wide earthquake of unprecedented severity (Rev 6.14 with 16.18). Somehow – and we are not told how – our Creator God will sustain life until He reverses the damage. Just as there is evidence from a careful study of Genesis that there were huge geological, climatic and environmental differences between the antediluvian and postdiluvian worlds, so there will be between the present age and the Millennial earth. Things are different in this planet before and after God's intervention in judgment.

The world's geography will be radically changed, starting with a great east to west valley which will be formed when Jesus' feet touch the Mount of Olives (Zech 14.4), with a river running in either direction from a mighty spring in Jerusalem (Zech 14.8). Other changed geographical features are foretold by several of the prophets. The Gulf of Aqaba or tongue of the Egyptian Sea will disappear completely (Isa 11.15). "Every valley shall be exalted and every mountain and hill brought low; the crooked places shall be made straight and the rough places smooth" (Isa 40.4). Why should some take this figuratively? The present topography is largely the result of the immense convulsions which took place beneath the waters of Noah's Flood, with some later glacial and other modifications. Some of the highest mountain ranges were once part of the sea bed. Is God incapable of doing this again? Of course not! Jesus told His disciples about faith to move mountains. This also is generally assumed to be figurative. But is it *really* beyond the bounds of possibility that some believers in their resurrection bodies may be given the task of rearranging the Millennial world?

The curse imposed upon the ground, which brought thorns, thistles and demanded hard labour (Gen 3.17-19), will be lifted. A proper relationship between humans and animals will be restored. There are wonderful descriptions to be found in Isaiah, eg 11.1-9, where we read of peace between wild animals and much more, and in chapter

35, where we learn that the desert shall rejoice and blossom as the rose. It will be on a scale far greater than anything seen hitherto in Israel, even with the help of artificial irrigation. In 49.10-12 we read of the equable climate and ease of communication. In Amos 9.11-15 we learn of amazing agricultural productivity and wonderful harvests. Indeed, promises of Millennial blessing are scattered widely throughout the Psalms and Prophets. From Isaiah 35 we know that deserts will disappear. Perhaps icecaps will do so as well.

In Rev 16.3, under the second Bowl judgment, we are told: "Every living creature in the sea died." Yet in Ezek 47.9-10 we are told of rivers and seas teeming with fish. God has restored wild life before; He can surely be trusted to do it again. Whether all species are restored is a question we cannot answer. We assume from palaeontology that dinosaurs and many other types were not re-introduced by God following the Flood, or if they were, they did not survive long. There may be similar adjustments. We are told that there will be climatic changes. "The light of the moon will be as the light of the sun and the light of the sun will be sevenfold... in the day that the Lord binds up the bruise of His people" (Isa 30.26). No doubt God will allow nature to adapt to this. It will not in any way be Heaven, but it will be very like Eden.

"Then the eyes of the blind shall be opened, and the ears of the deaf shall be unstopped, then the lame shall leap like a deer, and the tongue of the dumb sing" (Isa 35.5-6). We can now see even more clearly how Jesus at His first coming was presenting Messianic credentials through His miracles. He was performing in a representative way what will be universal in His future Kingdom. He healed the sick, maimed and blind, fed the five thousand, stilled the storm, rode an unbroken donkey into Jerusalem and did much, much more.

GLEANINGS OF THE FIRST RESURRECTION

"And I saw thrones, and they sat on them, and judgment was committed to them. And I saw the souls of those who had been beheaded for their witness to Jesus and for the word of God, who had not worshipped the beast or his image, and had not received his mark on their foreheads or on their hands. And they lived and reigned with Christ for a thousand years" (Rev 20.4). Walter Scott writes: "We gather that no saint in the coming crisis dies a natural death. He either lives through the period or is martyred" (Exposition of the Revelation of Jesus Christ). All the evidence we can find confirms this.

One cannot reasonably remain an Amillennialist or hold any similar 'ism' which sees a single resurrection and single judgment if one reads through the closing verses of Revelation 19 and opening verses of Revelation 20 with an open mind. Placing an artificial halt at the end of chapter 19 turns an eminently straightforward sequence of events into a desperate cover up to justify a doctrine which crept into the Church during the Dark Ages.

Chapter 20.4-5 tells us in the clearest possible terms of martyrs being raised from the dead and living on earth a thousand years before "the rest of the dead" live again. The distinction between the timing of these two resurrections could not be made clearer than it is here. The First Resurrection is for the saved and the Second for the unsaved. The fact that some scriptures do not differentiate between them and simply refer to the resurrection does not in any way negate those which do specify or imply one or the other, such as, "You shall be repaid (recompensed) at the resurrection of the just" (Lk 14.14); nobody will be recompensed in this manner at the resurrection of the ungodly!

The firstfruits and main harvest of the First Resurrection will have long been garnered in. The third and final phase is due to coincide with Christ's return; whether at the very moment or shortly after we are not told. This presents no problem; it simply means that some of the righteous (or those made righteous by Jesus' blood) will be raised before others. Here are the Tribulation martyrs, "They lived and reigned with Christ for a thousand years" (Rev 20.4). The word 'live' implies 'come to life'; thus they will now receive their resurrection bodies. Their number will have swelled since the souls of martyrs were seen at the fifth Seal (Rev 6.9-11); these had been told to wait until "the number of their fellow servants and their brethren, who were killed as they were, was completed". The perpetrators of their martyrdom will have been slain to await the Great White Throne; at last the victims will receive justice.

JUDGMENT OF LIFE AND SERVICE FOR REWARD AND RECOGNITION

Just as the Church will be judged in Heaven after the Rapture, so those martyred for their faithfulness, those who did not worship the Beast, will receive judgment for their service. This is not judgment for their sin – that was dealt with at Calvary, for it is said of them that they have washed their robes in the blood of the Lamb (Rev 7.14). One difference here is that there are a number of thrones, whereas at the Church's Bema or tribunal, Christ alone will judge. There will, we understand, be no previously resurrected saints to judge the Church, but there will be to judge the Tribulation martyrs, hence the multiplicity of thrones. Whether Jesus Himself occupies a central throne is not indicated. We rather think He will.

Perhaps the thrones are occupied by the same ones as are seen on the twenty-four thrones of Revelation 4; in Revelation 20 the number is not stated, so we are unsure. For Gentiles, probably resurrected believers other than the apostles will be appointed. There has been much speculation. One day we will see for ourselves.

Whoever occupies the thrones, surely it will be a wonderful sight, when those who during the Great Tribulation have resisted unto death for their Saviour are rewarded. Some may suffer some loss, like the least faithful of the Church at the Bema following the Rapture (I Cor 3.15), but this is doubtful with these saints, inasmuch as the cost of owning the name of Christ in the Tribulation period will be such that there are unlikely to be any half-hearted or semi-committed believers. Persecution is a wonderful purifier. Short term suffering or self denial can reap eternal dividends. The parable of the talents (Matt 25.14-30) has a special bearing on Israel, but it also illustrates the Lord's standards for recognition and reward for all believers.

Note that in Rev 20.4 there is no mention of the Church or any other non-Tribulation group to justify the Post-Tribulationist teaching of a late date for the Rapture.

RESURRECTION OF OLD TESTAMENT SAINTS

Strictly speaking the title 'Old Testament saint' applies to all who died with saving faith before Calvary. The first true New Testament saint was a criminal, crucified alongside Jesus when the New Covenant was sealed in His blood. Thus John the Baptist is an Old Testament saint, the Friend of the Bridegroom (Jn 3.29), rather than part of the Bride. The Old Testament saints are not mentioned in Revelation 20. Less is said about physical resurrection in the Old Testament than in the New, but it was firmly believed and taught except among the Sadducees. Martha, conversant with the Scriptures and speaking of her brother, said with confidence to Jesus, "I know that he will rise again in the resurrection at the last day". (Jn 11.24). Martha might have been thinking of any of the following passages:-

- "I know that my Redeemer lives, and He shall stand at last on the earth; and after my skin is destroyed, this I know, that in my flesh I shall see God" (Job 19.25-26).
- "Your dead shall live; *together* with my dead body they shall arise. Awake and sing, you who dwell in dust; for your dew is like the dew of herbs, and the earth shall cast out the dead" (Isa 26.19).
- "And there shall be a time of trouble, such as never was since there was a nation...Many of those who sleep in the dust of the earth shall awake, some to everlasting life, some to shame and contempt" (Dan 12.1-2). Then at the close of Daniel 12 the angel says to the aged prophet: "But you, go your way to the end; for you shall rest, and will arise to your inheritance at the end of the days" (v.13).

It is never actually stated in Scripture exactly when the Old Testament saints are to rise; even the Daniel 12 text above gives some scope. We must rely on inferences and deductions, and may not all come to the same conclusion. It could well be at that moment when the pierced feet touch down on the Mount of Olives. They would thus be able to see the fate of the trinity of evil and their followers.

The earliest option is that they ascended to Heaven with Jesus. An interesting statement in Matt 27.52-53, not enlarged upon elsewhere, is quoted in support of this. Some think that these Old Testament saints, who were raised after Jesus' resurrection and appeared to many in Jerusalem, were taken to Heaven by Jesus at His Ascension as a first sheaf of the First Resurrection harvest (Lev 23.10); this seems feasible, though the disciples saw only Jesus ascend. However Peter on the day of Pentecost, in other words after Jesus' Ascension, said quite specifically: "David is both dead and buried, and his tomb is with us to this day" and "David did not ascend into the heavens" (Acts 2.29 & 34); thus we are inclined to think that most if not all Old Testament saints are still in their graves.

Some believe that the Old Testament saints will rise with Church saints at the Rapture. As great authorities as JN Darby have suggested that the twenty-four elders of Revelation 4 (after the Rapture) will be the tribal patriarchs and the twelve apostles, and many since then have supported this idea. But Darby himself is not emphatic about this. Certainly the twenty-four names of the apostles and patriarchs are found together later in the New Creation (Rev 21.12-14). One feels that, were they to be raised after Christ along with the Tribulation martyrs, they would have been referred to in Revelation 20.

However there is another suggested timing worth considering. Tim La Haye quotes Dr Walvoord as saying that "the Old Testament seems to place the resurrection of Israel after the Tribulation. In Daniel 12, immediately after the description of the Tribulation in the preceding chapter, deliverance is promised to Israel..." He then refers to Dan 12.1-2, which we have also quoted. La Haye then adds: "The suggestion that Israel will be resurrected prior to the Tribulation saints results from a comparison of Rev:19.7-12 with Ps 50.1-6. At the marriage supper of the Lamb, Israel will be in attendance as friends of the Bridegroom. Since the marriage supper will occur just prior to the Glorious Appearing, we may assume that Israel will be resurrected *before* the Glorious Appearing, while Tribulation saints are raised during or at His Glorious Appearing." (Revelation Unveiled). We are inclined towards this view, but see merit in others. 'Wait and see!' is the best advice we can offer.

THE RESURRECTED REDEEMED IN THE MILLENNIUM
We rely mainly on the Old Testament for details of conditions for those who are in their mortal bodies during the Millennium, but we have to glean from verses scattered throughout the New Testament information regarding the life of the immortal saints.

We, the Church, are going to return to earth with Christ at His Coming in Power, and remain forever with Him. We will be witnesses of His glory, whether in Heaven or on earth. "I desire that they also whom You gave Me may be where I am, that they may behold My glory, which You have given Me" (Jn 17.24). "It has not yet been revealed what we shall be, but we know that when He is revealed, we shall be like Him, for we shall see Him as He is" (I Jn 3.2). Even the old apostle did not know all the details, but he did solemnly remind us in the next verse that this should be a purifying hope.

In his book 'The Scroll of Time' John Savage writes: "It is important to observe, that the rewards spoken of in Scripture are generally, if not exclusively, concerned with Christ's appearing and kingdom, and that *different* ones will be given according to the degree of faithfulness in service down here". When we read those passages which speak of conditional or earned honour, we should remember that the quality of our present service here is likely to determine our levels of responsibility during the Millennium. "And (You) have made us kings and priest to God; and we shall reign on the earth" (Rev 5.10). "If we endure, we shall also reign with Him" (II Tim 2.12). In the parable of the nobleman who went to the far country, the good servants are given authority over ten and five cities respectively when their master returns to receive his kingdom (Lk 19.11-27).

We shall be in our resurrection bodies, having, we believe, the same basic physical properties that Jesus had on earth between His Resurrection and Ascension. Will the Millennial inhabitants see us come and go through walls? Perhaps they will, but it is dangerous to see our roles in terms of science fiction. It is easy to let our imagination run riot and to see the Millennial kingdom as a two-tier society, where half of the population is bound by the limitations which we currently experience, but the other half is at liberty to appear and disappear suddenly like supernatural snoopers and invaders of privacy. We don't think it will be quite like that. Some commentators have suggested that the resurrected saints will be free to 'commute' between Heaven and earth; we reserve judgment on that.

What is much more important and reassuring is that we will have achieved that state which Paul longed for in his frustrating weakness (Rom 7.15-25). "For what I will to do, that I do not practise, but what I hate, that I do…It is no longer I who do it, but sin that dwells within me. For I know that in me (that is, in my flesh) nothing good dwells...O wretched man that I am! Who will deliver me from this body of death?" The whole passage should be read. Now of course this 'body of death' will be discarded for ever at the Rapture. "Our citizenship is in heaven, from which we also eagerly wait for the Saviour, the Lord Jesus Christ, who will transform our lowly body, that it may be conformed to His glorious body" (Phil 3.21).

When we celebrate the Lord's death at Breaking of Bread or Communion, we often quote Jesus' words: "I will not eat of this fruit of the vine from now on until that day when I drink it new with you in My Father's kingdom" (Matt 26.29). Jesus was not referring to Heaven, but to His Millennial kingdom, when the Twelve will be in or around Jerusalem. We know nothing about the anatomy of the celestial body, other than the fact that it is tangible, rather than ghostly (Lk 24.37-40 & Jn 20.27) and that one is able to eat earthly food (Lk 24.43 & Jn 21.13). As yet this is beyond our comprehension; then it will seem natural.

Our responsibility towards the mortal inhabitants of the Millennial earth may be akin to that of the angels towards us in our age. This does not mean that we are about to make those faithful spirit servants of God redundant, nor do we expect to grow wings! The emotional nonsense which sometimes appears in our press after the death of a child about becoming an angel is totally fallacious, though the implied fact that there is some belief in God is commendable. We probably owe angels immeasurably more than we realise. Speaking of man, the writer to the Hebrews, having talked about angels, writes: "But now we do not yet see all things put under him" (Heb 2.8). Apparently a great deal of authority, probably lost by Adam, is yet to be delegated to resurrected saints – particularly those who have proved themselves worthy. We may be sure that, whatever responsibilities we shall have, we will not be bored!

THE END OF THE YEAR OF MY REDEEMED
Reading Isaiah 65, we might get the impression that the Millennial Kingdom will go on for ever. Certainly the Kingdom will last forever (Dan 2.44), but it will not always be upon this earth. We are furnished

with more information in Revelation, as we have already seen, with the emphasised thousand years being followed by something entirely different in the new heaven and earth (Revelation 21 & 22). The earth, the atmosphere and the starry heaven – all that is currently visible - will come to an end. "The heavens and the earth which now exist are kept in store by the same word, reserved for fire until the day of judgment and perdition of ungodly men" (II Pet 3.7). God, who is infinite and bound neither by time nor light years, can wind all up in an instant. This is a reference neither to the Lord's return nor to Armageddon. It looks beyond the Millennium.

Rev 20.7-9 gives us a brief account of what will happen at the end of the Millennium; it seems very strange until we appreciate the reason for it. Satan must be released briefly. Those who have been born during the Millennium and who have never been truly born again, but who have harboured in their hearts resentment or rebellion against Christ's rule, will be tested. Millions will foolishly join in, and, in a re-run of the Gog and Magog rebellion of a thousand years before, will attempt to overthrow Jerusalem. A fire will come out of Heaven and destroy them. Then at last Satan will join his partners in the lake of fire. In the Millennium nobody can be saved without having had the option of choosing or rejecting Christ.

Christ's earthly rule will be over. He will have been glorified and vindicated in the world which once rejected, reviled and crucified Him. It cannot be otherwise. "Then comes the end, when He delivers the kingdom to God the Father, when He puts an end to all rule and all authority and power. For He must reign till He has put all enemies under His feet. The last enemy that will be destroyed is death" (I Cor 15.24-25).

We have completed our terms of reference and have viewed the last three chapters of the history of this old world, using the Bible as a guide. We have looked in some detail at The Day of Vengeance of our God and have seen how it relates to the longer periods before and after it. We have noted that the blackest chapter is much the shortest. However we have also seen that the two chapters of earth's history which lie ahead are both essential to God's plans and are demanded by His righteousness. But it would be irresponsible to leave it at that. We shall examine very briefly what happens when this creation has ceased to be, and we will look at the unique way, guaranteed by God, to "be counted worthy to escape all those things that will come to pass and to stand before the Son of Man" (Lk 21.36).

CHAPTER EIGHT

Eternity and Our Personal Destination

THE GREAT WHITE THRONE

We must deal with this dreadful matter before turning to the new heaven and earth, because that is the sequence in which we find them in the Bible.

"Then I saw a great white throne and Him who sat on it, from whose face the earth and the (visible) heaven fled away. And there was found no room for them. And I saw the dead, small and great, standing before God, and the books were opened. And another book was opened, which is the Book of Life. And the dead were judged according to their works" (Rev 20.11-12). There will be no redeemed present; they will all have participated in the First Resurrection, which culminated a thousand years earlier. This is the Second Resurrection; and the bodies will not be glorious, whatever assurances are sometimes given at funerals. Not only those in normal graves, but those whose remains have been scattered will be there, for the sea is said to give up its dead. Souls and spirits will be recovered from Sheol or Hades. Just as at the Rapture the human trinity of believers will be made complete (I Thess 5.23), so the unsaved will appear as body, soul and spirit to be judged individually by their Creator.

People will be judged in two ways. Present will be the Book of Life of the Lamb, where the lack of an entry will demonstrate failure to accept the salvation that had been on offer, thus excluding from Heaven and consigning to Hell. This solemn truth is often preached by evangelists. Neglect of salvation will be the paramount factor. Every knee sooner or later must bow at the name of Jesus (Phil 2.10); at this point this will be far too late to avail.

What is rarely taught, although it is plainly stated in Revelation 20, is that people are also to be judged according to their works. Works can never save, but are evidence of degrees of good or evil. Failure to teach this has led some to adopt the reasoning that if they are going to go to Hell anyway, there is no point in resisting temptation; they might as well commit whatever crime they wish, because, they wrongly think, it will make no difference in the end. This is folly.

The One who will then be seated upon the throne said long ago that it would be more tolerable for Sodom and Gomorrah and for Tyre and Sidon than for certain cities in Galilee (Matt 10.15; 11.22-24). Perhaps it is because of the sensitivity of the subject, that the Eternal Judge Himself makes these declarations, rather than delegating them to prophets or apostles, even though their writings were divinely inspired. There are evidently degrees of punishment; there are many hints of this in the Bible but no exposition or indication of how this will be achieved. We can only conclude that this is because God does not want us to use Scripture as a basis for gambling with eternal destinies. Being in the least awful place in Hell will be infinitely and inexpressibly worse than being in the humblest place in Heaven. There is no teaching in these or any other verses in the Bible of a temporary Purgatory or other means of earning a transfer from one place to the other. At the moment of physical death the data for the Judge's eternally binding decision will be finalised – utterly beyond reversal. Any other teaching has its roots elsewhere than in Christianity.

Hell or the lake of fire is as yet uninhabited. But it is the place where "their worm does not die, and their fire is not quenched" (Isa 66.24). Jesus told us that it has been prepared for the Devil and his angels (Matt 25.41), but those who reject a salvation never on offer to fallen angels will also be consigned there. Its everlasting status is qualified in Scripture in the same way as Heaven. It is not an enjoyable topic to write about; it is even more difficult to talk about.

THE NEW HEAVEN AND EARTH
Only those references which are not contained in Revelation 21 and 22 are given here; the others can be readily found within this most profitable of passages. "The day of the Lord will come as a thief in the night, in which the heavens will pass away with a great noise, and the elements will melt with fervent heat; both the earth and the works that

are in it will be burnt up...Nevertheless we, according to His promise, look for new heavens and new earth in which righteousness dwells" (II Pet 3.10, 13).

"And I saw a new heaven and a new earth, for the first heaven and the first earth had passed away" (Rev 21.1). It is strange that the New Heaven and New Earth of Revelation 21.1 to 22.15 should be considered less controversial than the thousand year duration of the millennial earth. Perhaps this is because it is easier to cope with something which is acknowledged to be hard to comprehend than it is to cope with something which is clearly and repeatedly stated in the Bible, but which may not fit in with our preconceptions.

One difficulty with the main Hebrew and Greek words for heaven is that they have to cover three concepts. In ancient times 'first heaven' applied to the atmosphere or firmament (as in Gen 1.9), 'second heaven' to the visible starry heaven (as in Ps 8.3) and 'third heaven' to God's dwelling place, which is, if we can describe it thus, on a different plane as part of a separate creation. Paul said "He is not far from each one of us" (Acts 17.27); and Jacob was shown a vision of a ladder with angels ascending and descending (Gen 28.12). Our present experience is of only one end of this communication link; one day we will understand. No Christian thinks twice about whether his or her prayers are heard in Heaven, though uttered on earth. The foretold destruction is of the first heaven and probably the second, but not of the third. The earth and visible heaven have to be replaced rather than restored; the Greek *poieo* implies that the new heavens and earth have to be made or constructed. This is one of the contrasts with the earlier Millennium with its divinely refurbished environment.

There is no hint in the Bible that the description is allegorical. It is factual, but presented in a way which will help us to accept the salient features. Of course there must be some interpretation here, and it is neither feasible nor necessary to reach a complete consensus over every detail. The geography, if we may use that term, is not the main information which has to be imparted, but we are given a few particulars, such as the absence of sea, and told of certain conditions about this new creation. Other imparted data may be specific only to the Holy City itself. Among the general facts, we are told that God's dwelling place will be there and that there will be neither death, nor sorrow, nor crying, nor pain.

The New Jerusalem is seen descending from God out of His Heaven. We believe that this is the place which Jesus went to prepare and to which He is to take us when He comes for us (Jn 14.3). Presumably therefore it will already have been inhabited by the Church after the Rapture. But Jesus has been preparing it for us since His Ascension, rather than only for the period between the Rapture and Coming in Power, so this is something which for the present is new to us. It has been suggested that during the Millennium resurrected saints will have access to it, though it will not at that time be visible from below. It will not descend to an earth which is bound for eventual destruction. When it descends to the new earth it will give access to all.

The age-old breach between Heaven and earth will at long last be closed. The Good News Bible says at Rev 22.15 that all manner of sinful things are "outside the city". This is one of many dreadful distortions of Scripture which have been introduced by 'reader-friendly' and casual translators and swallowed by an undiscerning public. Wholesale paraphrasing of Scripture is *bad* news as it is desperately subjective. The Greek *exo* simply means 'outside' and does not add the word for city. Evidently it indicates outside God's new creation rather than merely outside the city. Sin will be allowed neither in the New Heaven nor on the New Earth.

The City is so identified with the Church, the Lamb's Bride, that the two seem to be synonymous or at least inseparable. Israel will also have a part in the City, as the names of the tribes are inscribed on the gates, even as those of the apostles are on the foundations. Israel is described as the wife of Jehovah in Hos 2.16, a fact often ignored as we concentrate on the Church's status as the espoused Bride. It is to measure fifteen hundred miles in all three dimensions, forming, apparently, a perfect cube! This illustrates how very, very different this new creation will be from anything we have known. The city itself will not require the light of the sun, for God Himself is its light; there is to be no night there. This may or may not apply outside the city.

But perhaps the loveliest feature of all is the everlasting presence of the Lamb. The wonderful climax of the doctrine of the Lamb is at last revealed. This has spanned history from the time that Abel offered the acceptable sacrifice of the firstborn of his flock through the pages of Scripture. We think of some of the highlights, such as the substitute ram provided by God in place of the willingly offered Isaac; of the Passover lamb whose blood had to be shed and displayed to provide cover from judgment; of the lamb dumb before her shearers, which first disclosed that this was an actual person rather than a mere animal, and then of course the public identification of Jesus Christ at Jordan-side as the Lamb of God. But now we find that the Lamb is to retain His office and title throughout eternity, as the surest guarantee of the everlasting nature of our salvation. He is mentioned as the Lamb no less than seven times in those two final chapters of that wonderful book which liberals love to hate. I quote from the writings of my old pastor, based upon a marathon sermon which enthralled me as a teenager.

"How sublimely wonderful is this sevenfold relationship between the heavenly Bridegroom and that queen city of the new earth! How rapturously it lights up the indissoluble bond that binds the people of Christ to their Lord and Saviour! The Lamb is the Bridegroom and His people are the bride, so it is a *loving* union. The Lamb is both the temple and the object of His people's worship, so it is an *adoring* union. The Lamb is the luminary or eradiating glory light, so it is a *transfiguring* union. The Lamb is the portal and "nothing that defileth" can ever gain access, so it is a *holy* union. The Lamb is the life and we live in His life for ever, so it is a *life*-renewing union. The Lamb is the King and His people reign with Him for ever, so it is a *royal* union." (The Master Theme of the Bible, J Sidlow Baxter).

SIGNS OF THE TIMES

Too many Christians approach the signs of the times with an over-cautious "this is all very well, but..." attitude. The Bible does not provide us with a spoon-fed diet of pre-digested prophetic data. The signs of the times are presented in such a way that a strong element of faith must be added to the intellect, and the Pharisees whom Jesus addressed did not possess such faith. Even among believers faith may frequently waver. We are not talking of saving faith, but of the mature faith which is necessary to accept the more startling disclosures about God's latter day programme.

Even faith is insufficient; it must be accompanied by a love of our

Saviour. The signs of the times will have infinitely more appeal if, like the lover of the Song of Solomon (Cant 5.4-6), our heart truly yearns for our Beloved's footfall:

"I can almost hear His footfall on the threshold of the door,
And my heart, my heart is longing to be with Him evermore."

Of course if we don't believe in the Rapture, none of this will make much sense. Longing for death is not normally a virtue. If we believe in the Bible, we must believe in the Rapture, whatever we call it. We may be entitled to argue about the timing, but never about the basic facts.

The more comfortable we are in our Christian lives, the less likely we are to be interested. If we are in complacent, lukewarm Laodicean type congregations, which think that they are prospering and in need of nothing, we will have no interest in our Saviour's approach. If we are in Ephesian type congregations, which are burgeoning with activities but have lost their first love, we are likely to be equally disinterested, unless we are prepared to stand out from the crowd and risk unpopularity. These allusions are to the epistles of Revelation 2 and 3.

"Now when these things begin to happen, look up and lift up your heads, because your redemption draws near" (Lk 21.28). The Lord's return for us is signalled by the start of the signs, not by their end. The escalating signs are portents - grim shadows cast forward into the Acceptable Year by the lurid glow of the approaching Day of Vengeance.

The scoffers and the apathetic tend to be dismissive of the signs of the times, even though it was an expression used only by Jesus: "Hypocrites! You know how to discern the face of the sky, but you cannot discern the signs of the times" (Matt 16.3). This was in response to the request of the Pharisees and Sadducees for "a sign from Heaven". Here were men who claimed to honour the Holy Scriptures, and who were confronted by all the evidence fulfilling prophecy within Jesus' ministry, but who refused to believe without some science-fiction type of manifestation – something which would have dispensed with any need for faith, without which "it is impossible to please God". How history repeats itself!

Of course many of those evil things which we regard as signs of the near return of our Lord for us and of the coming Day of Vengeance have happened, at least in a limited way, in the past. Of course there are some good and encouraging things still happening. But when we put them all together and add them to those signs which are unprecedented, then we must take heed. Many of the signs which we are about to list have been mentioned and given Scriptural references in the text of this book. Here we are giving the very briefest description; some are more impressive than others. Please think long and hard before scoffing, particularly if you are in or influenced by one of those churches which teach that the world is being 'christianised' preparatory for the Lord's ultimate return.

Harbingers of coming environmental judgments:
- Global warming and melting ice caps.
- Increased hurricanes, tsunamis and floods.
- Growing desert and arid regions.
- Unpredictable growing and harvesting conditions.
- Many areas of famine and malnutrition despite scientific advances.
- Increasingly depleted fish stocks in seas and rivers.
- Fear of asteroid strikes.
- New diseases appearing as quickly as old ones are eliminated.
- God dishonouring religions fired by and inciting hatred, and rejoicing in inflicting pain.

International Depravity:
- Human ability to destroy all life on planet.
- Despite UN, NATO etc, numerous local wars.
- Genocide.
- Child soldiers and terrorists – incitement to hatred from the cradle.
- Inter-racial tensions, strife and hatred.
- People trafficking, mainly for prostitution, largely women and children.
- Slave trade, forced labour, child labour, debt bondage.
- Hindu caste system – 250,000,000 untouchables.

Degeneracy within 'Christendom' or "Christian nations":
- Equal status for all religions.

- Rejection of Lord's Day.
- Increasing legislation against evangelisation.
- Flaunting perversions which the Bible declares to be abominations.
- Overturning of Ten Commandments at European parliamentary level.
- The 'right' to practise immorality enshrined in law.
- Failure to balance human rights with human responsibilities.
- The right of the criminal greater than that of the victim.
- Denial of the status of human embryos which have bodies, souls and spirits.
- Departure from marriage as the norm, 'partner' status, one parent 'families'.
- Persistence in teaching evolution despite contrary evidence.
- Growth of Eastern mysticism, yoga, transcendental meditation and New Age.
- Horoscopes, tarot cards and allied occult devices more respected than the Bible; popularity of witchcraft novels.
- Escalation of Satanism in Europe, often initially through a mixture of black magic, hard drugs, sex and heavy metal.

Luke-warmness within churches:
- Ephesian type congregations, full of activities but with departed first love.
- Laodicean pride in unspiritual congregations with high opinions of themselves.
- Scoffing and apathy regarding Lord's return.
- A watered down Gospel with the 'threat' removed and doctrines marginalised.
- Worldliness within Church, blurred distinctions, lack of separation.
- Friendly overtures towards other "faiths".

Regarding Israel
- Israel's return to the Promised Land after almost nineteen centuries.
- The rebirth of a long dead language - Hebrew.
- Israel's survival against overwhelming military odds in 1948, 1967 and since, making a mockery of the rhetoric of Islam and exposing the falsehoods of the Koran.

- Israel already viewed as a "burdensome stone" for all nations.

GOD'S GUARANTEED ESCAPE ROUTE

"As I live, says the Lord, I have no pleasure in the death of the wicked, but that the wicked turn from his way and live. Turn turn from your evil ways!" (Ezek 33.11).

Christian preachers and writers, including those who have some specialisation in the field of prophecy, do not proclaim the need for salvation from a position of sinlessness; anything but. They preach from the standpoint of sinners saved by grace – by God's freely offered love for the undeserving. Perhaps the study of prophecy emphasises more than any other topic in the Bible our dire need for redemption, in view of the glorious future for those who receive it, and the unspeakable everlasting cost of rejecting it.

"Ho! Everyone who thirsts, come to the waters; and you who have no money, come and buy...without money and without price" (Isa 55.1). None of us has the currency to purchase our salvation and thus to acquire eternal life and a home in Heaven. Only one currency is acceptable with God the Father; and that is the shed blood of His Son, who, as the Son of Man, our Kindred Redeemer, died on an accursed cross. God tore Himself asunder when Christ laid aside His glory and "made Himself of no reputation, taking the form of a bondservant, and coming in the likeness of men" (Phil 2.7). The Father is glorified when we bow the knee to Jesus, when we confess that Jesus Christ is Lord (Phil 2.10-11). All must bow sooner or later at His name, before or after the grave, irrespective of creed, colour or status.

"Behold now is the accepted time; behold now is the day of salvation" (II Cor 6.2). The Acceptable Year of the Lord rapidly approaches its end; as individuals we do not know what a single day may bring forth. In the meantime the assurance is still there, that "All that the Father gives Me will come to Me, and the one who comes to Me I will by no means cast out" (Jn 6.37); this verse led the author to a saving faith in 1949! God has always known whether we as individuals will be saved or not; we cannot yet stand back in eternity to see how this can be; but the responsibility still remains with us. "Whom He foreknew, He also predestined to be conformed to the image of His Son" (Rom 8.29). Exercising our initiative in response to His initiative is critical.

Whatever our denomination, church membership cannot save us; neither can a Christian family background; nor can our own good works, no matter how upright we may be. In the matter of our salvation we may have nothing of which to boast or glory "except in the cross of our Lord Jesus Christ" (Gal 6.14). On the other hand, no criminal record will disqualify the truly repentant sinner who believes.

And for those who have accepted Jesus Christ as Lord and Saviour, the prophetic word still carries a message of warning, though in this case not so dire. As we have seen in such passages as I Cor 3:10-15 and II Cor 5.10-11, it is possible to be saved as surely and securely as the brightest saint, but to appear empty-handed and ashamed before Him at His coming (I Jn 2.28). The shame would be were we to have nothing to bring, no crown to cast at His feet, no tangible tribute to present to Him.

> The bride eyes not her garment,
> But her dear bridegroom's face.
> I will not gaze at glory,
> But on my King of grace;
> Not at the crown He giveth,
> But on His pierced hand.
> The Lamb is all the glory
> Of Immanuel's land.

Anne Ross Cousin's peerless words assume the award of a crown. But may you expect one? May I?

"The Spirit and the bride say, 'Come!' And let him who hears say, 'Come!' And let Him who thirsts come. And whoever desires, let him take the water of life freely" (Rev 22.17). This gracious invitation has an RSVP; if we fail to respond, we cannot expect to find a place reserved for us. If we have replied and accepted, we will, when we hear Him say, "Surely I am coming quickly", be able to reply, "Amen. Even so, come Lord Jesus!" (Rev 22.20).

In the meantime there is work to be done for the Lord; a battle to be fought. In the words penned with a background in the American Civil War and the days of semaphore, we say:

> "'Hold the fort, for I am coming!'
> Jesus signals still:
> Wave the answer back to heaven,
> 'By thy grace we will!'"

"The grace of our Lord Jesus Christ be with you all. Amen." (Rev 22.21).

Glossary of Terms

This is for quick reference. All these terms are explained and their sources given within the text of the book.

Acceptable Year of the Lord   The age inaugurated by Jesus at the outset of His ministry, spanning the Church Age and ending with the Rapture (qv).

Amillennialism   The belief that there will be no literal thousand year rule of Christ upon earth, but rather that the present Church Age is the Millennium. Many variations exist; held by liberals and evangelicals alike. Many Replacement Theologians (qv) are Amillennial.

Abomination of Desolation   A detestable, blasphemous image of the Beast which is to be set up in the Jerusalem temple at the mid-point of the 70th heptad (qv).

Antichrist   The most commonly used, though not the most accurate, name for the **Man of Sin**, the Beast, **The Son of Perdition** etc. The satanically inspired superman and arch-deceiver, who will emerge as leader of the ten nation confederacy, or Revived Roman Empire at the start of the 70th heptad (qv). He will be recognised by many Jews as the Messiah and will conclude a 7 year treaty with them, breaking it after 3½ years, when he will desecrate the temple, claim to be God and demand universal worship. He will lead the satanic armies at Armageddon (qv). He will be consigned to the **Lake of Fire** when Jesus returns in power. Other minor antichrists have existed through the ages.

Armageddon, Battle of   The demon driven concentration of the world's armies to confront God at the end of the Great Tribulation. Centred in Northern Israel but extending as far as Jerusalem. Jesus Christ will intervene in glory and utterly destroy them.

Beast   See Antichrist

Beginning of Sorrows   The first half of the Tribulation (qv).

Bema The Judgment Seat of Christ in Heaven for the Church, following the Rapture (qv). Lives, works and service for the Lord will be evaluated in the way that precious metals are tested by fire. The fire thus applies to the works and in no way suggests any purgatory. Individuals may be rewarded by a variety of crowns or other marks of recognition, accompanied by great joy. Others may be left empty handed and ashamed. Believers' sins were, of course, judged in Christ at Calvary and are therefore not taken into consideration.

Coming in Power   The visible return of the Lord Jesus Christ as King of Kings and Lord of Lords – King and Judge – at the end of the Day of Vengeance to execute judgment upon Satan, the Beast, the False Prophet and their armies and to fulfil everything necessary to usher in the Millennium (qv) or Year of the Lord's Redeemed. Jesus will be followed by the armies of Heaven – saints and angels.

Day of Vengeance of our God   Equates to the Tribulation period (qv)

Diaspora   Greek term – that which is sown – the name applied to the Jews living outside Palestine and maintaining their religious faith away from the Gentiles.

False Prophet   Also described as the **Second Beast**; this is the evil being who supports and directs worship towards the Beast. He will possess miraculous powers, will enforce the Mark of the Beast (qv) and is destined for the Lake of Fire at Christ's return.

Great Tribulation, The   The second half of the Tribulation (qv) and unprecedented time of suffering for the world.

Great White Throne The judgment following the Millennium, the end of this world and the second resurrection, for the unsaved only – those whose names are not written in the **Lamb's Book of Life**.

Heptad   Any group of seven. Applied to the seventy groups of seven or 'weeks' of years, 490 years in all, prophesied in Daniel 9. The first 69 heptads expired when Jesus was rejected as Messiah. One remains to be fulfilled after the Rapture (qv), though not necessarily starting at that moment.

Lebensraum   Territory which the Germans believed was needed for their natural development.

Mark of the Beast   A mark, perhaps an implant, to be worn on the right hand or forehead early in the Great Tribulation (qv), without which it will be virtually impossible to buy or sell goods. In order to receive it, the holder must swear allegiance to the Beast, and thus indirectly to Satan. For this reason those who receive it will place themselves beyond salvation.

Millennialism Sometimes called **Chiliasm**. The belief in a literal thousand year rule upon earth of Jesus Christ, marked by righteousness, peace and a restored environment.

Millennium The thousand year rule of Christ on earth following the Battle of Armageddon, interpreted literally by Millennialists and either figuratively or loosely by many others. Latin for 1,000 years.

Mystery Babylon   A blasphemous religious organisation or false church; guilty of the blood of the martyrs. Often associated in the past with Rome, but in its final form more likely to be a conglomerate of apostate Christianity and paganism, with its headquarters either at Rome or Babylon. Satan and the Beast will make use of it, but will ultimately disown and destroy it as they crave direct worship.

NU   The eclectic Greek text in the twenty-sixth edition of the Nestle-Aland New Testament (N) and in the third edition of the United Bible Societies' Greek New Testament (U).

Post-Millennialism The belief that Jesus will not return to earth until the end of the Millennium, which may or may not imply the present age, and that the Church will or should bring about ideal moral conditions for this return. Very wide in its scope. Ignores or plays down any Day of Vengeance. Some Replacement Theologians are Post-Millennial.

Pre-Millennialism The belief that the Church will be raptured and that Jesus will return to earth before the Millennium. Most but not all Pre-Millennialists believe that the Rapture will occur before the Tribulation period. Held exclusively by evangelicals.

Preterism The teaching that most or all latter day promises have already been fulfilled. Many think that events surrounding the destruction of Jerusalem comprised the Great Tribulation (qv). Totally reliant on many prophecies being highly exaggerated for effect. Uncommon among evangelicals.

Rapture The collective snatching or catching up to meet the Lord in the air of the newly resurrected bodies of the dead in Christ and the translated bodies of the living saints, with onward progress to Heaven.

Replacement Theology The teaching that, since their rejection of their Messiah, the Jews have no present or future place in God's plans and that the Church has eternally inherited all the blessings and privileges (but apparently not the curses!) accorded to Israel.

Revived Roman Empire, The (see also Times of Gentiles) Earth's final rebellious empire. Its head of government or emperor will be the Beast. It has to be smashed by Christ at His coming and superseded by His everlasting kingdom, which will initially be earth centred. Its capital, in the light currently available to us, seems more likely to be Rome than Babylon.

Seals, Seven Seals of a scroll to be opened in Heaven by Jesus Christ in His offices as the Lamb that had been slain, Lion of the Tribe of Judah and Root of David. Each Seal is a heavenly trigger or authorisation for events on earth during the Tribulation; they will include the **Four Horsemen of the Apocalypse**, and will institute two series of seven judgments by sounding **Trumpets** and pouring out **Bowls of Wrath**; these take us to the point of Christ's Coming in Power (qv).

Times of the Gentiles Announced by Daniel in his interpretation of King Nebuchadnezzar's dream and confirmed to be on-going by Jesus Himself in His Olivet Discourse. A succession of five Gentile empires were to dominate the world around Israel and occupy that

Land. These were Babylon, Medo-Persia, Greece and Ancient Rome followed by a long time interval and the final yet future reappearance of Rome as the Revived Roman Empire. They end at Christ's Coming in Power.

Tribulation The 70th heptad (qv) before the Return of Christ in power. Split into two halves; which are variously described in Scripture as 1,260 days, 3½ years, 42 months and 'times, time and half a time'. The first half may be referred to as 'the Beginning of Sorrows; the second and more severe half as 'The Great Tribulation' or 'Time of Jacob's Trouble. The word 'tribulation' when not pre-fixed by 'the' refers to any period of trial.

Year of the Lord's Redeemed Equates to the Millennium, but with a special emphasis on Israel.

Bibliography

American Tract Society Dictionary, Power Bible, Phil Lindner Online, 2002.

Anderson, Sir Robert; *Daniel in the Critic's Den,* details not currently available.

Baines, TB; *The Revelation of Jesus Christ,* 4th edn, Gute Botschaft Verlag, 1991 reprint.

Barnhouse, Dr Donald Grey; *Revelation, An Expository Commentary,* Zondervan, 1971.

Baron, David; *The Visions and Prophecies of Zechariah,* Messianic Testimony reprint, 2000.

Baxter, Dr J Sidlow; *Explore the Book,* vol 6, Marshall, Morgan & Scott, 1955.

Baxter, Dr J Sidlow; The *Master Theme of the Bible,* Tyndale House Publishers, 1973.

Benware, Dr Paul; *Understanding End Times Prophecy,* Moody Press, 1955.

Boettner; Dr Loraine; *Fatal Error of Pre-Millennialism,* details not currently available*.

Cameron, Dr Donald CB; *Apocalypse Facts and Fallacies,* Twoedged Sword, 2006.

Darby, John Nelson; *Prophetic* vols II & IV, G Morrish, nd.

Ellicott, Dr Charles J; vol VI, *A Commentary for English Readers,* Cassell & Co, nd.

Henry, Matthew; *Commentary,* Marshall, Morgan & Scott, 1960 edn.

Ironside, Dr Henry H; *Revelation,* Loizeaux Brothers, revised edn, 1996.

Jamieson-Fausset-Brown Commentary, Power Bible, Phil Lindner Online, 2002.

Kelly, William; *Notes on Ezekiel,* G Morrish, nd.

Kelly, William; *Lectures on the Revelation,* G Morrish, before 1907.

King, Rev Geoffrey R; *Daniel – A Detailed Explanation,* The Midnight Cry, 1957.

La Haye, Dr Tim; *Revelation Unveiled,* Zondervan, 1999.

Lindsay, Rev Hal; *There's a New World Coming,* Coverdale House, 1973.

Miller, Dr EJ; *The Final Battle,* New Wine Press, 1987.

Pentecost, Dr J Dwight; *Thy Kingdom Come,* Victor Books, 1990.

Pollock, Algernon J; *Things Which Must Shortly Come to Pass,* Bible Truth Publishers, 1936.

Richards, Dr Lawrence O; *Expository Dictionary of Bible Words,* Marshall Pickering, 1985.

Ryrie Dr Charles C; *Revelation New Edition,* Everyman's Bible Commentary, 1996.

Savage, John Ashton; *The Scroll of Time,* Kingston Bible Trust/Chapter Two, 1982 reprint.

Scott, Walter; *Exposition of the Revelation of Jesus Christ,* Pickering & Inglis, 4th edn, nd.

Scroggie, Dr W Graham; *A Guide to the Gospels,* Pickering & Inglis, 1948.

Seiss, Dr Joseph A; *Lectures on the Apocalypse,* Charles C Cook, 1865.

Showers, Dr Renald; *Article in Your Tomorrow,* Prophetic Witness Movement Int, Feb 1993.

Tatford, Dr Frederick A; *The Climax of the Ages,* Oliphants Ltd, 1953.

Unger, Merrill F; *Unger's Bible Dictionary,* Moody Press, 3rd edn 1966.

Walvoord, Dr John F; *The Revelation of Jesus Christ,* Moody Press, 1989.

Walvoord, Dr John F; *Major Bible Prophecies,* Victor Books, 1990.

Young, Dr Robert; *Analytical Concordance,* Lutterworth Press, 8th edn, 1939.

* Similar statements may be found in Boettner's book, *The Millennium,* Presbyterian and Reformed Publishing Company, 1957.